WILDE

in an hour

BY EMILY ESFAHANI SMITH

SUSAN C. MOORE, SERIES EDITOR

PLAYWRIGHTS in an hour
know the playwright, love the play

IN AN HOUR BOOKS • HANOVER, NEW HAMPSHIRE • INANHOURBOOKS.COM
AN IMPRINT OF SMITH AND KRAUS PUBLISHERS, INC • SMITHANDKRAUS.COM

With grateful thanks to Carl R. Mueller, whose fascinating introductions to his translations of the Greek and German playwrights provided inspiration for this series.

Published by In an Hour Books
an imprint of Smith and Kraus, Inc.
177 Lyme Road, Hanover, NH 03755
inanhourbooks.com SmithandKraus.com

Know the playwright, love the play.

In an Hour, In a Minute, and Theater IQ are registered trademarks of
In an Hour Books.

The excerpts printed in this book are in the public domain.

Front cover design by Dan Mehling, dmehling@gmail.com
Text design by Kate Mueller, Electric Dragon Productions
Book production by Dede Cummings Design, DCDesign@sover.net

ISBN-13: 978-1-936232-30-7
ISBN-10: 1-936232-30-8
Library of Congress Control Number: 2009943223

CONTENTS

CONTENTS

Why Playwrights in an Hour?

This new series by Smith and Kraus Publishers titled Playwrights in an Hour has a dual purpose for being: one academic, the other general. For the general reader, this volume, as well as the many others in the series, offers in compact form the information needed for a basic understanding and appreciation of the works of each volume's featured playwright. Which is not to say that there don't exist volumes on end devoted to each playwright under consideration. But inasmuch as few are blessed with enough time to read the splendid scholarship that is available, a brief, highly focused accounting of the playwright's life and work is in order. The central feature of the series, a thirty- to forty-page essay, integrates the playwright into the context of his or her time and place. The volumes, though written to high standards of academic integrity, are accessible in style and approach to the general reader as well as to the student and, of course, to the theater professional and theatergoer. These books will serve for the brushing up of one's knowledge of a playwright's career, to the benefit of theater work or theatergoing. The Playwrights in an Hour series represents all periods of Western theater: Aeschylus to Shakespeare to Wedekind to Ibsen to Williams to Beckett, and on to the great contemporary playwrights who continue to offer joy and enlightenment to a grateful world.

Carl R. Mueller
School of Theater, Film and Television
Department of Theater
University of California, Los Angeles

Introduction

I think it is significant that Oscar Wilde, surely among the most elegant and accomplished masters of the English language, was an Irishman. In this, he joins a long list that, in theater alone, includes the greatest comic writers in literature, among them William Congreve, Oliver Goldsmith, Richard Brinsley Sheridan, Dion Boucicault, and, preeminently, George Bernard Shaw. (The Irish literary army that has conquered the English stage since Wilde is equally commanding, among them John Millington Synge, Sean O'Casey, Samuel Beckett, Brian Friel, and Martin McDonagh.)

What accounts for this flood of Irish comic writers on the English lit reading list? One could argue that it is partly a class and partly an ethnic phenomenon — namely the result of being an occupied people trying to overcome a sense of alienation in an imperialist world. In his life, as well as in his work, Wilde was both a conformist and an outlaw, whose art, as Emily Esfahani Smith rightly concludes in the suggestive essay that follows, "simultaneously reinvigorates and rejects society."

Gently satirized by Gilbert and Sullivan in the opera *Patience* as an aesthete in knee breeches carrying a green carnation, Wilde pretended to be devoted entirely to hedonistic pleasure. (He once urged his readers to "resist everything but temptation.") A married man with strong homosexual tendencies, he was willing to admit to effeminacy but never to gayness, which he called "the love that dare not speak its name." (Today's gay population has largely overcome that inhibition.) This reservation made Wilde commit a major tactical error after the Marquess of Queensbury, the father of his lover, Lord Alfred Douglas, had referred to him as "Oscar Wilde, posing as a Somdomite." Despite the ignorant misspelling, Wilde sued the thickheaded aristocrat for libel and lost the case, thereby exposing himself to prosecution and imprisonment for sodomy.

Moisés Kaufman has chronicled this tragic decline of an extraordinary career in his play *Gross Indecency: The Three Trials of Oscar Wilde*. But apart from some musings in his long essay *De Profundis* (1905), Wilde left the subject untouched. Instead, he mainly devoted his writing life to a series of light well-made sentimental comedies — among them *Lady Windemere's Fan* (1892), *An Ideal Husband* (1895), and *A Woman of No Importance (1893)*. Were it not for their extraordinary dialogue, these plays would be no better remembered than the plays of Arthur Wing Pinero. Apart from his novel about the physical consequences of moral corruption, *The Picture of Dorian Gray* (1890), it is for his one-act biblical drama, *Salomé* (1891), and particularly for that delicious masterpiece of the absurd, *The Importance of Being Earnest* (1895), that Wilde has earned his reputation as one of the great Victorian writers. Surely, the character of Lady Bracknell remains unequalled as a portrait of smug English Philistinism.

Curiously, George Bernard Shaw was among the few critics to belittle Wilde's comic achievement, probably because Shaw believed it to be insufficiently socially engaged. The irony is that *The Importance of Being Earnest* is one of the most subversive works in the English language. It is certainly the best embodiment of Wilde's dandy aesthetic.

Ultimately, Oscar Wilde was his own work of art. His capacity to carve his extraordinary persona into monuments of frivolity is what has made this Irish wit one of the supreme English dramatists of all time.

Robert Brustein
Founding Director of the Yale and American Repertory Theatres
Distinguished Scholar in Residence, Suffolk University
Senior Research Fellow, Harvard University

Wilde

IN A MINUTE

AGE	DATE	
—	1854	**Enter Oscar Fingal O'Flahertie Wills Wilde.**
1	1855	Walt Whitman — *Leaves of Grass*
3	1857	Irish Republican Brotherhood founded with intent to establish an independent Ireland.
5	1859	Charles Blondin crosses Niagara Falls on a tightrope.
11	1865	Lewis Carroll — *Alice's Adventures in Wonderland*
13	1867	World Fair in Paris introduces Japanese art to the West.
16	1870	First Vatican Council establishes doctrine of papal infallibility.
17	1871	Franco-Prussian War ends with German victory.
18	1872	James McNeill Whistler — *The Artist's Mother*
20	1874	British Major Walter C. Wingfield popularizes lawn tennis.
21	1875	Roller-skating rinks debut in London.
23	1877	Henrik Ibsen — *The Pillars of Society*
24	**1878**	**Wilde's poem "Ravenna" wins the Newdigate Prize at Oxford.**
26	**1880**	**Oscar Wilde — *Vera; or, The Nihilists***
27	1881	Chat Noir, the first cabaret, opens in Paris' Bohemian Montmartre district.
28	1882	The U.S. bans Chinese immigrants for ten years.
29	**1883**	**Oscar Wilde — *The Duchess of Padua***
30	1884	Divorce is reestablished in France after a sixty-eight-year ban.
32	1886	Friedrich Nietzsche — *Beyond Good and Evil*
34	1888	George Eastman perfects his Kodak camera.
36	**1890**	**Oscar Wilde — *The Picture of Dorian Gray***
37	**1891**	**Oscar Wilde — *Salomé***
38	**1892**	**Oscar Wilde — *Lady Windermere's Fan***
39	1893	George Bernard Shaw — *Mrs. Warren's Profession*
40	1894	Baron de Coubertin begins organizing modern Olympic Games.
41	**1895**	**Oscar Wilde — *The Importance of Being Earnest***
42	1896	Alfred Nobel dies, founding Nobel Prizes in his will.
43	1897	Havelock Ellis — *Studies in the Psychology of Sex*
44	**1898**	**Oscar Wilde — *The Ballad of Reading Gaol***
46	**1900**	**Exit Oscar Wilde.**

A snapshot of the playwright's world. From historical events to pop-culture and the literary landscape of the time, this brief list catalogues events that directly or indirectly impacted the playwright's writing. Play citations refer to premiere dates.

Wilde

HIS WORKS

DRAMA

Vera; or, The Nihilists
The Duchess of Padua
Lady Windermere's Fan
A Woman of No Importance
La Sainte Courtisane
A Florentine Tragedy.
Salomé
An Ideal Husband
The Importance of Being Earnest

FICTION

The Canterville Ghost
The Happy Prince and Other Tales
The Picture of Dorian Gray
Lord Arthur Savile's Crime and Other Stories
A House of Pomegranates
Poems in Prose

POEMS

"Requiescat"
"Ravenna"
Poems
"The Sphinx"
The Ballad of Reading Gaol

This section presents a complete list of the playwright's works in chronological order.

ARTICLES, ESSAYS

"The Rise of Historical Criticism"

"The Critic as Artist"

"The Decay of Lying: An Observation"

"The Soul of Man under Socialism"

"Phrases and Philosophies for the Use of the Young"

De Profundis

Onstage with Wilde

*Introducing Colleagues and Contemporaries
of Oscar Wilde*

THEATER

William Archer, Scots playwright and critic
Herbert Beerbohm Tree, English actor
Sarah Bernhardt, French actress
Anton Chekhov, Russian playwright
Henrik Ibsen, Norwegian playwright
John Millington Synge, Irish playwright
Eugene O'Neill, American playwright
August Strindberg, Swedish playwright

ARTS

Paul Cézanne, French painter
Edward Burne-Jones, English Pre-Raphaelite painter
Vincent van Gogh, Dutch painter
Modest Mussorgsky, Russian composer
Pierre-Auguste Renoir, French painter
John Singer Sargent, American painter
George Gilbert Scott, English architect
Richard Wagner, German composer

POLITICS/MILITARY

Alexander II, Russian czar, emancipator of serfs
Otto von Bismarck, Prussian statesman
Isaac Butt, Irish nationalist politician
Benjamin Disraeli, British prime minister
Charles Stewart Parnell, Irish nationalist leader

This section lists contemporaries whom the playwright may or may not have known.

Theodore Roosevelt, American president
Queen Victoria, British monarch
Kaiser Wilhelm II, German emperor, king of Prussia

SCIENCE

Alexander Graham Bell, Scottish inventor
Karl Benz, German engineer
Marie Curie, French chemist
Charles Darwin, English naturalist
Havelock Ellis, English psychologist
Sven Hedin, Swedish explorer
Max Planck, German physicist
J. J. Thomson, English physicist

LITERATURE

Matthew Arnold, English poet and essayist
Henry James, American novelist
John Ruskin, English professor, ethicist, and literary critic
Alfred, Lord Tennyson, English poet
Leo Tolstoy, Russian novelist
Ivan Turgenev, Russian novelist
Paul Verlaine, French poet
Walt Whitman, American poet

RELIGION/PHILOSOPHY

Karl Barth, Swiss theologian
Karl Marx, German socialist philosopher
John Henry Newman, English cardinal
Friedrich Nietzsche, German philosopher
Pope Pius IX, Italian pope
Grigori Rasputin, Russian monk
Herbert Spencer, English philosopher
Hippolyte Taine, French philosopher

SPORTS

Richard Brown, American captain of the sailing yacht *Americ*
Alexander Joy Cartwright, American baseball player
Charlotte Cooper, English tennis player
James J. "Gentleman Jim" Corbett, American boxer
Pierre de Coubertin, French founder of modern Olympics
W. G. Grace, English cricketer
James Naismith, Canadian-born American inventor of basketball
Margaret Scott, English golfer

INDUSTRY/BUSINESS

Andrew Carnegie, Scottish industrialist
George A. Fuller, American inventor of the skyscraper
King Camp Gillette, American businessman and inventor
William Kellogg, American industrialist and founder of the
      Kellogg Company
J. P. Morgan, American financier and banker
Joseph Pulitzer, Hungarian-American publisher
Cecil Rhodes, English businessman
John D. Rockefeller, American industrialist

WILDE

in an
hour

INTRODUCTION

On October 10, 1854, Oscar Fingal O'Flahertie Wills Wilde was
delivered to a world ill equipped for his wit, genius, and drama. Full of
inconsistencies, this Victorian era aesthete spun the drama of his life
and the conflicts of his world into plays that are still hailed as master-
pieces today — plays that prove his point that "a truth in art is that
whose contradictory is also true," as reported by Richard Ellmann, his
foremost biographer. Nothing delighted this dandy more than the rib-
ald contradictions that swirled around Europe at the end of the century. Wilde, in his comedic and subtle attack on both individuals and
the society they formed, promoted an individualism that railed against
the tyranny of dictators, societies, and religion. He believed that the
artist's mission was to create beauty and confront injustice and to do so
with a flourish. Wilde's own life was full of flourishes, though those
societal contradictions he hilariously exposed in his plays would ultimately lead to his own undoing. Wilde's enthusiasm that art simultaneously reinvigorates and rejects society remains the underlying theme of
both his life and his plays — genius, sensitivity, and frivolity shaking a
rigid world loose. That, at least, was the plan.

This is the core of the book. The essay places the playwright in the context of his or her world and analyzes the influences
and inspirations within that world.

HISTORICAL AND SOCIETAL CONTEXT

The Victorian world provided fodder for Wilde's imagination and his plays. Born in 1854 in Ireland, he died in 1900 in France — a year before Queen Victoria herself passed away. In Britain, the Victorian era was defined by rapid change: the Industrial Revolution, mass consumption, urbanization, and the creation of new social classes. Pushing back against these societal changes, the Victorians tried to assert values of propriety and decorum and maintain a semblance of the traditional aristocratic order. But this task became increasingly difficult as radical philosophical, intellectual, and artistic movements did away with the old in favor of the new.

In a political essay titled "The Soul of Man under Socialism," Wilde attacked Victorian society and identified himself as a socialist and an individualist. The contradictions of his own political beliefs are expressed through Mrs. Erlynne in *Lady Windermere's Fan*: "I am so much interested in his political career. I think he's sure to be a wonderful success. He thinks like a Tory, and talks like a Radical, and that's so important nowadays."

Wilde explored the capacity of art to influence the course of society during a time of dynamic change at the turn of the century — philosophically with Nietzsche, economically with Marx, psychologically with Freud, historically with Hegel. In his art, Wilde set out to discover a remedy for a society poisoned by hypocrisy.

FAMILY LIFE

Wilde's father, Sir William Wilde, was Ireland's foremost ear and eye surgeon and was knighted for his accomplishments. In addition, he wrote books on medicine, archaeology, and folklore. In 1851, he married Wilde's mother, Jane Francesca Agnes Elgee. Before her marriage, Elgee wrote revolutionary poems and articles for the Young Ireland movement, which were published in *The Nation* under the pseudonym Speranza. One of her pieces, calling for armed revolution in

Ireland, drew the attention of the British authorities, who shut the newspaper down.

Oscar Wilde had an elder brother, William "Willie" Charles Kingsbury, and a younger sister, Isola Emily Francesca. Isola's childhood death of meningitis greatly affected Wilde. He wrote a poem, "Requiescat," dedicated to her memory and carried with him always a lock of her hair sealed in an envelope. Willie lived in the shadow of his younger brother with great resentment, which eventually undermined their relationship. Wilde also had three half siblings — a brother Henry and two sisters, Emily and Mary, born from affairs his father had before his marriage to Elgee. The two half sisters died tragically in a fire while in their early twenties.

Wilde was particularly close to his fiery nonconformist mother, Lady Jane Francesca Wilde. Lady Wilde was the archetype for a Wildean woman. An Irish nationalist, she was blessed with high intellect and had a passionate interest in culture. The family lived in fashionable digs on Merrion Square in Dublin where Lady Wilde hosted Saturday afternoon salons, during which intellectuals, politicians, and socialites gathered for witty repartee and enlightened discourse.

Wilde's attachment to his colorful mother is evident in the letters he wrote to her from school, one of which, quoted in Ellmann's biography of Wilde, details the budding dandyism that would bloom fully in later years: "The flannel shirts you sent in the hamper are both Willie's, . . . [mine are] quite scarlet and the other lilac but it is too hot to wear them yet."

SCHOOLDAYS

Both Wilde and his brother Willie attended the Portora Royal School in Enniskillen, Ireland — a preparatory school for Trinity College similar to Eton, Oxford's preparatory school. Wilde excelled, winning top prize in the classics. He went on to Trinity College on a Royal School Scholarship, where he shared a room with Willie. He excelled at Trinity as well, placing first in his examinations and winning a Foundation

Scholarship. He also won the college's Berkeley Gold Medal for Greek, the highest award for Greek students, and was awarded a Demyship scholarship to Magdalen College in Oxford. While at Magdalen, Wilde won the 1878 Newdigate Prize for his poem "Ravenna."

While at Magdalen College, Wilde perfected the persona he would present to the world. He defied the authorities in matters both high and low, personal and political. He deliberately dropped his Irish accent for an educated English one and took to dressing in red silk and wearing his hair long, as he mockingly denounced "manly sports." His room was decorated with blue china, sunflowers, lilies, and peacock feathers. According to Ellmann in his biography, Wilde became notorious for lamenting, "How often I feel how hard it is to live up to my blue china."

He drew so much attention to himself that campus publications accused him of being a poseur. His room was repeatedly vandalized, and legend has it that a college sports team dunked him in a nearby river at the prompting of a professor. Through his individualism, he expressed his contempt for authority.

At Magdalen, Wilde began his studies of classical literature and philosophy. Included was the classicism of Aeschylus, the idealism of Plato, the realism of Aristotle, and the romanticism of Keats and Blake. Inquisitive and introspective as he was, Wilde soon applied his learning to the question of how to live his own life. To devote himself to a life of pleasure and art would be his initial strategy and was implemented for most of his life.

But Wilde's aestheticism involved more than the adoration of blue china and suiting up in plum-colored breeches and silk stockings for the balls at Magdalen. Wilde believed that art can reinvigorate society. When at Oxford, he wrote in his notebook in French, "beauty is perfect / beauty is capable of all things / beauty is the only thing in the world which does not excite desire." Yet he was overwhelmed and ultimately undermined by his insatiable appetite for pleasure.

Eventually, he was also drawn to religion. His mother's son to the end, he rejected the Protestantism of Anglican England in favor of the romantic Catholic Church. Religion became a complex issue for Wilde during his classical training. Wilde's two mentors at Magdalen gave shape to this struggle: Walter Pater, an aesthetic ethicist, and John Ruskin, a Christian ethicist. The opposing views of these two formidable intellects delineated Wilde's own spiritual conflict as he tried to reconcile the two belief systems. During Wilde's life, Pater won out in the struggle for his intellect. Late in life, after having been imprisoned for the crimes of indecency and sodomy, a lonely and despondent Wilde sought out a copy of Pater's *The History of the English Renaissance* for consolation. But Wilde's soul was forever being drawn back to Ruskin.

THE AESTHETIC MAN VERSUS THE ETHICAL MAN

On the one hand, there was the infinite potential of human imagination, intellect, and creativity and on the other, solace in penitence and the redemption of his soul. Wilde's vision of unlimited human potential encouraged him to indulge his moods and passions; whereas his need for comfort and relief from distress led him to the inner peace gained from self-sacrifice and prayer. One promised infinite awareness while the other demanded humility and poverty.

As a youth, Wilde was attracted to the aesthetics of Catholicism: its ceremonies and rituals, its candles and incense, its devotional scenes and pietas. The aesthetic trappings of the Catholic Church are there to inspire the devotee to accept the perfect goodness and charity of Christ, but to Wilde, the aesthetic experience is the end. To him, art itself is an expression of the infinite.

A close Catholic friend, David Hunter Blair, made an effort to convince Wilde of the eternal truth of Catholicism. He arranged for Wilde to have an audience with Pope Pius IX. After meeting the pope, Wilde locked himself in his rooms, emerging only after writing a sonnet inspired by and dedicated to Pius. Ellmann reports in his biography that on that same day, when Blair and Wilde stopped at the Protestant cemetery in Rome where John Keats was buried, Wilde knelt at Keats' grave and announced it to be "the holiest place in Rome." The devout Blair, infuriated at this blasphemy, would later tell Wilde, "You will be damned. You will be damned for you see the light and do not follow it."

For Wilde, rejecting Catholicism was a practical and temporary matter: He decided to exercise his imagination now and to worry about his soul when his time on earth was running out. Now he would indulge himself with the beauty of this life, rather than the vague possibilities of what might lie beyond. In *De Profundis*, Wilde expanded on the theme of self-realization, "I don't regret for a single moment having lived for pleasure. I did it to the full, as one should do everything that one does. There was no pleasure I did not experience. I threw the pearl of my soul into a cup of wine. I went down the primrose path to the sound of flutes. I lived on honeycomb. But to have continued the same life would have been wrong because it would have been limiting. I had to pass on. The other half of the garden had its secrets for me also."

In Wilde's soul, the aesthetic man and the ethical man were at odds. His two great mentors at Oxford represented those dualities: Pater is the aesthetic man, and Ruskin is the ethical or just man. Aesthetic man surrenders wholly to his feelings in an effort to fully realize his potential. In so doing, aesthetic man moves from sensation to sensation. This puts an obstacle between what he wishes and hopes to be and what he actually is. Ethical man is much more disciplined and constrained, operating under a value system that seldom depends on passion and sensual delight. Sensual delight and indulgence are signs of weakness in this system. Ethical man recognizes that he wants his soul to be good, not necessarily fully realized, and it is this goodness to which he attains. Going to church, enjoying and understanding art, reading scriptures — these are all methods by which ethical man elevates his soul, aspiring to the perfect goodness embodied in God.

Wilde's imagination was certainly drawn to a pious Catholicism. "I will seek the shelter of a Church which simply enthralls me by its fascination," he would say according to Pearce. At some point, Catholicism negates the superiority of the human intellect in favor of divine intellect and knowledge through the grace of God. Yet, Wilde thought that to deny the supremacy of the intellect was to deny the progress of the soul "from darkness to darkness," Ellmann reported in the book he edited about Wilde. No, Wilde would follow the flame instead, even if that light contained dangers.

Wilde would always carry with him, both in his own life and in the lives he created for his plays, Pater's words: "Success in life is to burn always with this hard gemlike flame." So, to burn is to live life. And how to burn with the brightest flame? For Wilde it is the aesthetic life that burns the brightest. And so it was that the aesthetic man dominated the ethical man in Wilde's inner struggle. Not until he lay on his deathbed did Wilde accept the Christ of Catholicism, and so at the end, he passed on from this earth with the ethical man in control.

LONDON AND LOVE

After graduating from Magdalen in 1878, Wilde returned to Dublin where he met and fell in love with Florence Balcombe. Though the two exchanged romantic letters, Balcombe became engaged to Bram Stoker, the author of the novel *Dracula*. Upon hearing this, Wilde, in full dramatic form, declared that he would leave Ireland forever. He moved to London 1879 with his friend Frank Miles, a high-society portrait painter.

In 1880, Wilde's first play *Vera; or, The Nihilists* was published. It was scheduled for production, but was cancelled at the last moment because it was deemed too controversial. In 1881, he published his first collection of poetry, called simply *Poems*, which received mixed reviews.

In May of that same year, Wilde met Constance Lloyd, whom he would later marry in 1884. She was well read, spoke several European languages, and had an independent mind. She was the daughter of the rich and esteemed council to the queen, Horace Lloyd. Though Wilde swore his love to Constance Lloyd, expressions of devotion both during courtship and marriage were mostly offered by her. She bore him two sons, Cyril in 1885 and Vyvyan in 1886. The marriage included a 250-pound annual stipend, which afforded Wilde the aesthetic and luxurious life that he desired. An aspect of this lifestyle were forays back to his arcadia, Oxford. On one such trip, in 1885, barely a year into marital bliss, Wilde met young Robert Ross, who seduced Wilde, making him realize the truth about his sexuality. Ross also introduced him to the tempestuous Lord Alfred Douglas, who was to become a major figure in Wilde's life.

THE CREED OF AESTHETICISM

Late in 1881, Wilde set sail for New York City and traveled across the United States on a fifty-lecture tour on aesthetics, originally scheduled to last four months. The tour wound up lasting nearly a year, with over 140 lectures given in 260 days.

The series of lectures he delivered across America, which would make him famous, brought order and form to his many disparate thoughts on aestheticism. Entitled "The Artistic Character of the English Renaissance," the series was Wilde's first effort at defining aestheticism before a receptive and curious public. Zukowski reports that he said, "Aestheticism is a search after the signs of the beautiful. It is the science of the beautiful through which men seek correlation of the arts. It is, to speak more exactly, the search after the secret of life." During the sober nineteenth century, aestheticism was a radical creed to embrace.

Wilde craved this beauty throughout his life: through his work and through his love of women first and then of men. Wilde conducted his search for the pure idea and form of beauty — platonic in the first instance — in the here and now, that is to say in the flesh and all that it entailed. When on trial for sodomy and indecency, according to Ellmann in his biography, he described this thirst for beauty as the "love that dare not speak its name." By this he meant the perfect love between an older man and a younger man. When pressed at his trial to articulate exactly what such a love entails, Wilde spoke with characteristic eloquence and beauty: "It is that deep spiritual affection that is as pure as it is perfect. It dictates and pervades great works of art, like those of Shakespeare and Michelangelo, and those two letters of mine, such as they are. It is in this century misunderstood, so much misunderstood that it may be described as the 'Love that dare not speak its name,' and on account of it I am placed where I am now. It is beautiful, it is fine, it is the noblest form of affection. There is nothing unnatural about it. It is intellectual, and it repeatedly exists between an elder and a younger man, when the elder man has intellect, and the younger man has all the joy, hope and glamour of life before him. That it should be so the world does not understand. The world mocks at it and sometimes puts one in the pillory for it."

AESTHETICISM CORRUPTED BY EXCESS

In 1883, when Wilde made a formative trip to Paris, he would find his aestheticism followed to its earthly conclusion. That conclusion was unwholesome and often decadent. In those years, he embraced homosexuality and indulged the impulses of his passions, both sensual and emotional. Harry Marillier, a boy whom Wilde tutored, was one of the first young men for whom Wilde felt a romantic inclination. Ellmann reports in the book he edited, that in a letter to Marillier, Wilde wrote, "Sometimes I think that the artistic life is a long and lovely suicide, and am not sorry that it is so." He foresaw his own destruction as his ideal aestheticism swerved into decadence. Indeed, he would give advice along these lines to André Gide, according to Ellmann — advice that, when Wilde himself took it, led to his own self-destruction: "Nothing is good in moderation. You cannot know the good in anything till you have torn the heart out of it by excess." Ironically, Wilde claimed that self-denial was the primary way in which progress is arrested. Yet by indulging his desires, the destruction of his self followed — not the creation of art.

Wilde's aesthetics are complex because they attempt to describe a complex world. Wilde thought that people who followed the conventions of Puritanism and Victorianism lost the capacity for beauty and art; they preferred to live a life of repression and simplicity. Wilde used the theater to sort out the details of his aesthetics. As Ellmann writes, "By the time he left the university [Magdalen] he could see that life's complexity could not easily be codified into thirty-nine or even forty-nine articles, into ten or twenty commandments, into pluses and minuses awarded to this person or that creed. Wilde was a moralist, in a school where Blake, Nietzsche, and even Freud were his fellows. The object of life is not to simplify it. As our conflicting impulses coincide, as our repressed feelings vie with our expressed ones, as our solid views disclose unexpected striations, we are all secret dramatists. In this light, Wilde's works become exercises in self-criticism as well as pleas for tolerance."

Even Wilde himself understood the inconsistency of his nature. With one turn of phrase he would hail such an inconsistency as artistic truth and by another he would decry as reported by Ellmann in the book he edited, "With every breath of thought I am weaker and more self-deceiving than ever."

As Wilde's own literature foretells in the dark deeds of Dorian Gray and the frivolous Algernon Moncrieff, one cannot confuse the ideal in all its otherworldly perfection with the real. Transcendent beauty is adulterated by the physical world. It was precisely the physical component of his heterosexual and homosexual love that left Wilde at a loss.

In Wilde's only novel, *The Picture of Dorian Gray* (1890), Dorian Gray is an exceptionally beautiful young man and the subject of a portrait by artist Basil Hallward. Through Basil, he meets Lord Henry Wotton, who convinces him to lead a hedonistic life devoted to pursuing beauty and pleasure. In an effort to preserve his youth and beauty, Dorian sells his soul so that only his portrait will age, while he will remain ageless. His aesthetic pursuit of the senses leads him to debauched and cruel acts, including murder. In the end, wracked by fear and guilt, he attempts to destroy the portrait, slashing it with a knife, and instead dies, his face and body finally registering his true age and corrupt condition. Dorian was determined to indulge in more sensual pleasure than a single soul could possibly experience. The result of his excessive indulgence of the aesthetic impulse is degeneration and death. By indulging his aesthetic impulses at the expense of his ethics and conscience, Dorian, in glorious pursuit of beauty, kills himself. In many respects, Dorian's quest and ultimate destiny anticipates Wilde's.

VICTORIAN DRAMA AND WILDE

Wilde's plays followed the model of the well-made play, which was the fashion in London's West End theater district. These plays followed a predictable formula that upheld the ethical, moral, and romantic suppositions of the time. First, the key characters of a play are introduced, often by minor figures such as servants, who discuss the affairs of their masters. Then a dramatic situation arises in which the characters misunderstand a crucial part of the dramatic action. Next the misunderstanding is taken to its logical end. In a concluding scene, the different viewpoints are reconciled, producing a harmonious resolution.

Among Victorian playwrights, there were two groups: Those who followed the established plot formula, and those who varied from its structure. George Bernard Shaw denounced the assumptions on which these plays were based as false, and he replaced them with his own point of view. Wilde, on the other hand, took the absurdities of Victorian society on its own terms and created a well-made play. But through the use of language, epigrams, and comedy, he turned high-society's "truths" upside down. His were conventional plays filled with an unconventional ethic. Though he adhered to the form of a well-made play, the essence of his plays revealed a morality grounded in charity and redemption.

THE INFLUENCE OF IBSEN

Victorian drama was heavily affected by the introduction of the plays of Henrik Ibsen onto the London stage in 1889. Peter Raby reports that the performance of *A Doll House* in London that year caused Harley-Granville Barker, an actor, to recall, "It was the most important dramatic event of the decade." While Ibsen was praised for the social modernity and piercing individualism of his characters, critic Herbert Beerbohm Tree wrote that Ibsen's plays were "an admirable manure for the future, a dunghill from which many a fair flower of the drama may bloom."

Ibsen often wrote tragedies about middle-class individuals that were full of tension and earnestness. In style, they were the opposite of Oscar Wilde's jovial society comedies. Strangely, William Archer, the dramatic critic and playwright, argued for the merit of Ibsen and realism on the stage, yet he declared Wilde, whose plays were quite different from Ibsen's, as on "the highest plane of modern English drama." as quoted by Wilde in his book *The Plays of Oscar Wilde*. While not writing in the same tradition, Wilde was deeply struck by the gravity of Ibsen's plays. They shared some common themes. Wilde attacked the hypocrisy of Victorian high society and its morality. In Ibsen, Wilde saw the idea that once individuals bound themselves to social codes, the codes would conflict with the virtues they were meant to serve: securing human happiness.

VERA; OR, THE NIHILISTS

Wilde turned his gaze to politics with his first play, the unsuccessful *Vera; or, The Nihilists* (1880). Though Ellmann in his biography quotes Wilde as saying that *Vera* is "a play not of politics but of passion," the political current of the play drives the passion. Politically, *Vera* confuses socialism with republicanism. The nihilists seek the overthrow of the tyrannical czar in the name of liberty before considering the implications of their revolutionary zeal. Vera, their heroine, is the only nihilist who realizes that she is caught in the intersection between political ideology and passionate realism.

Vera was inspired by an actual event that occurred in St. Petersburg on March 24, 1878. On that day twenty-two-year-old Vera Ivanovna Zasulich, in a dramatic assassination attempt, shot the chief of police, General Fyodor Fyodorovich Trepov. The wound was not mortal. Though she did not deny her guilt, she was acquitted and found "not guilty."

At the beginning of the prologue to the play, Vera is worried about her brother Dmitri who has gone off to Moscow. By prologue's end, she has transformed into a nihilist, committed to avenging his downfall. The prologue takes place during the night, when Vera discovers that Dmitri has been taken to a labor camp in Siberia where torture and death await him. The first act closes as Vera reads a message from Dmitri containing the nihilists' oath: "to strangle whatever nature is in me; neither to love nor to be loved; neither to pity nor to be pitied; neither to marry nor to be given in marriage till the end is come."

In the next act, which jumps five years into the future to 1800, a nihilist parley is just beginning in Moscow. Vera has become a popular revolutionary icon, the police are after her, and the czar himself fears her influence. She is a heroine to and inspiration for the nihilists who have come to Moscow to plan the assassination of the czar and, in so doing, foment regime change. The police, having discovered the plot, encourage the czar to declare martial law. The conspirators believe that martial law, if implemented, "will be the death warrant of Russia."

Alexis, the son of and soon-to-be successor to the czar, is among the assassins who will do the deed. He has long despised the cruel governance of his father and supports the nihilist cause.

When the nihilists discover that Alexis is heir to the throne, they immediately make him public enemy number one and put him at the top of their hit list. They draw lots to award the job, and Vera wins the "honor." She and Alexis have become lovers, and now Vera must choose between her love of Russia and her love for Alexis, an apparently impossible choice. But, without hesitation, she shouts, "The lot is mine! See the bloody sign upon it! Dmitri, my brother, you shall have your revenge now."

But when Vera, intent on her murderous mission, arrives at the palace and sees Alexis, she is overwhelmed by feelings of love. The lovers exchange vows of deep and lasting love, even as the conspirators gather outside the window, expecting Vera to throw them a dagger stained with Alexis' blood to prove that the act is done. Absent this sign of mission accomplished, they will rush in and kill him themselves. As Vera realizes that it grows late, she panics and acts to save her beloved Alexis: She stabs herself, inflicting a mortal wound, and hurls the dagger, dripping red with her own blood, from the window. Her final words are "I have saved Russia."

In self-sacrifice, Vera brings the virtue of love to politics — sacrificing herself so that Alexis may live on for her and for Russia. Like Wilde, when Vera is challenged by opposing forces, she chooses both, confident that Alexis' life will not only be an continued expression of her love for him but will also save Russia. In Vera's final act, Wilde explores an emerging concept of his aesthetics: That in art, the opposite of a "truth" may also be true.

If Wilde was correct that the play is in the passion, it is worth looking at the various ways in which passion drives the play. When Vera makes a speech denouncing martial law to the nihilists and proposing the assassination of the czar, she appeals to a sense of humanity that is defined by its passions: "O God, how easy it is for a king to kill his people by thousands, but we cannot rid ourselves of one crowned man in Europe! What is there of awful majesty in these men which makes the hand unsteady, the dagger treacherous, the pistol-shot harmless? Are they not men of like passion with ourselves, vulnerable to the same disease of flesh and blood similar our own?" Vera understands all men are subject to passion, king and commoner alike, but that she is now directed by love, a higher power.

Vera and Alexis have escaped the prison of their passions, in which the czar and the nihilists, whose passions have corrupted them, remain. The czar, upon learning that his son is a nihilist, declares "war against the people." From his uncontrolled passion, springs paranoia, cruelty, murder, despair, and ultimately his own destruction. Wilde draws a contrast between the ennobled death of Vera, driven by love, and the crazed and useless death of the czar.

When *Vera; or, The Nihilists* was staged in New York, it was poorly received. *The New York Times* wrote, "it comes as near to failure as an ingenious and able writer can."

SALOMÉ

Salomé (1891) may be Wilde's most aesthetic play in its dependence on language and setting to create mood. The play was written in French, at the height of Paris' decadent art scene. Later, it was translated into English by Alfred Douglas, Wilde's lover.

Salomé is often called a symbolist play. Symbolist theater aspires to propel theatergoers to a higher spiritual plane and, once there, to inspire them to meditate on such transcendent forces as life's mysteries and the internal struggle for the sacred in a world of the profane. In *Salomé*, Wilde places uncontrollable sexual desire alongside spiritual piety to create a magnificent example of symbolist theater.

Found in the Gospel of Matthew, the story of Salomé recounts the beheading of John the Baptist by King Herod at Salomé's request. The prophet, called Iokanaan in Wilde's *Salomé*, is confined in a prison chamber near enough to King Herod's court for his prophecies to be overheard by the attendants, Salomé, her mother, and King Herod himself. "I hear in the palace the beating of the wings of the angel of death" is only one of his accurate prophesies.

Salomé's sexual advances to Iokanaan are spurned by the prophet — he resists her entreaties to kiss his mouth. King Herod, who in turn lusts after Salomé, repeatedly asks her to dance for him. She steadfastly refuses until he tells her he will grant her whatever she asks of him, even if her wish is half his kingdom, if she will only perform the dance of the seven veils. She agrees to dance, and it's then that the beautiful Salomé plots her revenge against Iokanaan. After her performance, she tells Herod that she wants the head of Iokanaan. Herod is initially horrified but delivers nonetheless; he has given his word, after all. Revolted by Salomé, he then has her killed. The theme of killing that which one loves for personal satisfaction is dramatized in this play.

At the beginning of the play, the imagery of the moon and that of Salomé are constantly confused, giving the reader the sense that Salomé is the moon itself. Later, Herod will say, "She is like a mad woman, a mad woman who is seeking everywhere for lovers." Though he is talking about the moon, his statement is equally applicable to his stepdaughter Salomé. Some contradictions begin to surface here. The moon comes to symbolize a type of madness and hysteria. This is paradoxical given that the moon is serene and silvery. The beauty of Salomé, too, inspires madness. "Your beauty troubled me," Herod tells her — though beauty typically is a source of transcendence and peace. Even Herod's page realizes the danger of earthly beauty when he chides the young Syrian, "You are looking at her. You look at her too much. It is dangerous to look at people in such a fashion. Something terrible may happen." This is the same way that Herod looks at her, and the way that she looks at the prophet. Indeed, the page's prophecy is being realized.

There is a poisonous relationship between death and desire in *Salomé*. Salomé represents the sensual beauty of this world and the flaming desire it ignites in men who see her. Herod's lust for Salomé leads to her death and indirectly to the prophet's. For Salomé, beauty and purity are intertwined, but she sees purity only in the physical, a fatal flaw. Wilde unites spiritual beauty and physical beauty at the end of the play when Salomé kisses the dead and pallid lips of the prophet. But at this moment, the stars disappear into an eerie darkness, and the moon's light cannot penetrate the clouds that cloak it, leaving only darkness onstage. At this moment the spotlight shines on Salomé, and Herod orders, "Kill that woman!"

Though it may be tempting to conclude that Wilde put Salomé and Iokanaan — the sin of passion and Christian virtue — on a similar moral plane since evil causes both to retire from the world, the reader should remember that the world of Iokanaan is located beyond the world of Salomé, which is this world, earth. It is Salomé, then, who is being indicted and Iokanaan who is being rewarded with his passage into a higher world. Herod, in watching this, has become repulsed by Salomé, and he has been made morally aware of her sin — the sin she inspired in his own heart.

Salomé was never staged in London in Wilde's lifetime. The Lord Chamberlain banned it from the stage citing a sixteenth-century law prohibiting dramatization, onstage, of religious and biblical themes. Even morality plays like the comparatively tame *Everyman* were denied a license for the playhouses in Wilde's time. Neil McKenna writes that this made Edward F. S. Pigott, the licensor of plays, wonder aloud why Wilde would submit his "half Biblical, half pornographic" play for a license. Perhaps Ellmann holds the answer in his biography of Wilde: "Wilde wanted a consuming passion; he got it and was consumed by it." Salomé as well.

THE SOCIETY COMEDY

Wilde's most successful form of drama was the society comedy, of which he wrote four: *Lady Windermere's Fan* (1892), *A Woman of No*

Importance (1893), *An Ideal Husband* (1895), and *The Importance of Being Earnest* (1895). Several features of these plays recur. Structurally, they begin with an exposition, which introduces the characters and setting while establishing the dynamic between the various characters, which may or may not evolve as the play proceeds. The characters are all located in a fashionable part of London or in a lavish country house. At this point in the play, all is well. The drama begins when a complication of some sort is introduced. This complication, through a series of interactions with the different characters, snowballs into a full-blown crisis that is resolved by the ebullient dandy of the play.

In these comedies, Wilde typically establishes a social network with rigid rules. He then points out the hypocrisy and contradictions within this society through humor. It is usually the dandy who is responsible for revealing truths of this sort. He also pokes at society by having a puritanical character led into viciousness and debauchery through the practice of her own rigid beliefs — this character is typically a woman.

The Dandy's Language

The most distinguishing feature of the dandy is his irrepressible language. The dandy is the master of philosophical epigrams. Everyone associates these witticisms with Oscar Wilde: "Arguments are to be avoided; they are always vulgar and often convincing." "Fashion is a form of ugliness so intolerable that we have to alter it every six months." "I think that God in creating Man somewhat overestimated his ability." "A man's face is his autobiography. A woman's face is her work of fiction." "I can resist everything except temptation." "Every woman is a rebel and usually in wild revolt against herself." Many of these epigrams are introduced in one play, and then reused in others. Wilde often used and reused epigrams, entire portions of dialogue, and imagery as a method to state, echo, and reecho vital truths.

In language, Wilde also establishes moral order. He juxtaposes his fresh epigrams with stale hackneyed phrases. In doing so, he challenges audience members in their perception of which characters are good or likeable and which bad or unlikeable. The dandy of the play is often a villain, yet a riveting one. The good people are often dull and unbearably obtuse in their clichéd existences. Wilde's dramatic sense made him realize that people with pasts make for interesting characters and therefore good drama. As Cecil Graham says in *Lady Windermere's Fan*, "Wicked women bother one. Good women bore one. That is the only difference between them."

The Dandy's Wisdom

During the exposition and complication period of the play, the dandy is detached from the moral crisis and is therefore able to comment lightheartedly on the drama going on around him. Whenever the dandy does become involved in the drama — during the crisis, when his wisdom is desperately needed — he loses his triviality, becomes serious, and resolves the crisis. Upon easing the tension, the dandy sometimes resumes his post as the in-house charmer of the play. Usually, the drama alters his nature in a profound way. For instance in *An Ideal Husband*, the instant the dandy Lord Goring understands what is troubling Lady and Sir Chiltern's relationship, he loses his gaiety. This can be seen in his uncharacteristically serious remarks like, "Robert, how could you have sold yourself for money?" Merely one act before, Lord Goring was commenting frivolously to Mabel, the object of his affection, "My father told me to go to bed an hour ago. I don't see why I shouldn't give you the same advice. I always pass on good advice. It is the only thing to do with it. It is never of any use to oneself." Then, by the time the curtain falls, the once-detached bachelor is now engaged to be married and about to enter into society formally, which means that he must give up his trivial and comic musings.

In essence, the dandy maintains a distance between himself and the real world, allowing himself to be above it and to make his life a work of art. Perhaps Wilde is compelled to make the point that only art can solve the many problems of the world, since the dandy is simultaneously the aesthete-in-residence and doctor of each play.

Occasionally, a woman is the dandy. In *A Woman of No Importance*, Mrs. Allonby's wit and magnetism are on par with Lord Illingworth's. And Mabel Chiltern of *An Ideal Husband* delights in sharing witticisms with her lover, Lord Goring. Sometimes, the dandy says what he means, like Lord Darlington. Other times, he is merely a cynic whose dandyism is a pose, like Lord Illingworth or Lord Wotton of *The Picture of Dorian Gray*. Although *The Picture of Dorian Gray* is a novel, it works the questions and answers of life in much the same way as Wilde's dramas.

The Fallen Woman

The sort of crisis that the dandy resolves typically involves a woman with a past. To have a past was the kiss of death in Victorian society, since it implied debauchery, waywardness, and many other social improprieties. In *Lady Windermere's Fan*, the woman with a past is Mrs. Erlynne, who fled from high society as a young woman, abandoning her daughter and husband in the process. This was all for the love of another man — who in turn abandoned her. Typically, it is a mistake of passion that exiles these fascinating women from society, and quite often the object of the play is their spectacular readmission into society. At other times, the purpose of the play is to show the consequences of their inevitable exile. Wilde criticized Victorian society for the hypocrisy that punished social impropriety as sinful in one person and yet ignored actual wickedness of conscience and character in another. As immoral as Mrs. Erlynne's action may seem, she is cast out of society because she represents a disorderly threat to its harmonious structure not because she is herself by nature bad.

Traditionally in Victorian literature, a drama about a fallen woman or man reaches its resolution by the ejection of that character from society by a respectable figure, typically a man. In Wilde's society comedies, the fallen figure is the creator of her own fate and even of her own salvation, if she indeed chooses to reenter society, like Ms. Erlynne in *Lady Windermere's Fan*, or decides to remain on its fringes, like Lady Arbuthnot in *A Woman of No Importance*. This is the individualism that Wilde brings to the table.

LADY WINDERMERE'S FAN

Lady Windermere's Fan (1892) was Wilde's first society comedy and his first successful play. Wilde wrote about this play, "If there is one particular doctrine contained in it, it is that of sheer individualism. It is not for anyone to censure what anyone else does, and everyone should go his own way, to whatever place he chooses, in exactly the way that he chooses."

Wilde declared his libertarianism to the world with this play. In it, he showed how individuals can be the craftsmen of their own fates — whether that fate ends in salvation or damnation, since both are viable alternatives. For instance, within this play of insiders and outsiders, Lord Darlington, one of the two outsiders, is willing to rupture the marriage of the hero and heroine, Lord and Lady Windermere, to make love to Lady Windermere. He begs her to leave London with him, which would ruin her socially. In this, he is operating under the false assumption that Lord Windermere has himself been unfaithful to Lady Windermere. Lord Darlington's many misjudgments result in exile from a society that could tolerate his passions or his deceptions.

Mrs. Erlynne is then, in some sense, the opposite of Lord Darlington. Her wit and compassion trump her social and moral transgressions and preserve her place in society. Even though Wilde believed that a person can act to save him- or herself, in his poem "Humanitad" he suggests that self-betrayal is an equally likely choice. This choice enlivens the moral drama in *Lady Windermere's Fan* as well. Lord Darlington begins in society and ends in exile, while Mrs. Erlynne begins in exile and ends in society. Both their outcomes are the result of their choices, affirming Wilde's individualism. As Lord Darlington implores Lady Windermere, "There are moments when one has to choose between living one's own life, fully, entirely, completely — or dragging out some false, shallow, degrading existence that the world in its hypocrisy demands. You have that moment now. Choose! Oh, my love, choose!"

The action of *Lady Windermere's Fan* takes place at Lady Windermere's birthday ball. Lady Windermere has been led to suspect her husband of an adulterous relationship with Mrs. Erlynne, an infamous woman whom the husband invites to the ball, to the horror of Lady Windermere. Lady Windermere swears, in puritanical outrage, to strike Mrs. Erlynne with a fan that was given to her as a birthday gift by her husband if the immoral woman dares to enter her house. Mrs. Erlynne is a "woman with a past," an outcast from society. Lord Windermere is financially beholden to her, and he is engaged in a peculiar effort to help her reenter the society she despises. Mrs. Erlynne is a very real threat to both the societal order, since she is entering it from outside the social circle, and to the internal order of Lord and Lady Windermere's marriage. And it is for this that all involved are naturally and deeply suspicious of her.

Contrary to what Lady Windermere believes, there is no romantic connection between Lord Windermere and Mrs. Erlynne. On the contrary, Lord Windermere hates Mrs. Erlynne and what she stands for. He is helping her only on the condition that she does not reveal her dark secret, a revelation that would humiliate his wife, Lady Windermere: Mrs. Erlynne is Lady Windermere's disgraced mother. Of course, Lady Windermere knows none of this. It all comes to a boil when Lady Windermere decides to flee London with Lord Darlington, the dandy who is in love with her. She flies to his house to enter his disastrous embrace. She waits for him in his rooms, as he has not yet returned from that evening's society ball, the last of the season, and likely the last of her life. Mrs. Erlynne, upon discovering Lady Windermere in his rooms, risks it all to save her daughter, imploring her not to leave the loving husband and child who are waiting at home for her. In short, she does not want her daughter to repeat the mistake that she herself made years past.

The two women start to exit Lord Darlington's rooms, when they hear the men approach, among them Lord Darlington, Lord Windermere, and Lord Augustus, whom Mrs. Erlynne is in love with. The two women hide, but Lady Windermere neglects to take her fan, which the men soon discover. Lord Windermere quickly recognizes the fan as his wife's. He angrily demands to know if Lord Darlington has hidden her somewhere. Before Lady Windermere can be discovered, Mrs. Erlynne sacrifices herself, her future, and her impending marriage to Lord Augustus by revealing herself and claiming the incriminating fan as her own. Of course, the implication is that Lord Darlington has received Mrs. Erlynne into his rooms for the seediest of reasons. In the confusion, Lady Windermere slips away unseen.

The two characters who undergo Wilde's dramatic transformation are, of course, Lady Windermere and Mrs. Erlynne. Wilde's criticism of Puritanism is that it causes Lady Windermere to act as she does. Lady Windermere begins the play, "My mother died when I was a mere child. I lived always with Lady Julia, my father's elder sister, you know. She was stern to me, but she taught me what the world is forgetting, the difference that there is between what is right and what is wrong. *She* allowed of no compromise. *I* allow of none." Lord Darlington challenges her moral rigor with, "Do you know I am afraid that good people do a great deal of harm in this world. Certainly the greatest harm they do is that they make badness of such extraordinary importance. It is absurd to divide people into good and bad. People are either charming or tedious."

Wilde drives home his criticism of Puritanism by having Mrs. Erlynne, the fallen woman, save the morally stifled Lady Windermere.

Lady Windermere's Puritanism breaks down when she goes to Mrs. Erlynne and holds "out her hands to her, helplessly, as a child might do" and asks Mrs. Erlynne to take her from Lord Darlington's rooms, to take her back to her own child. Lady Windermere sees that morality is multifaceted when she instructs her husband, "I don't think now that people can be divided into the good and the bad as though they were two separate races or creations. What are called good women may have terrible things in them, mad moods of recklessness, assertion, jealousy, sin. Bad women, as they are termed, may have in them sorrow, repentance, pity, sacrifice."

For Mrs. Erlynne, the transformation is also moral: In her expression of maternal love, she proves that she has learned from her past mistakes. When the audience discovers she is Lady Windermere's mother, she cries out, "Life doesn't repeat its tragedies like that! . . . The same words that twenty years ago I wrote to her father! and how bitterly I have been punished for it! No; my punishment, my real punishment is tonight, is now!" The most touching statement she makes in the play is about her grandson, Lady Windermere's son, whom Lady Windermere is about to abandon, "Go back to that child who even now, in pain, or in joy, may be calling to you. God gave you that child. He will require from you that you make his life fine, that you watch over him. What answer will you make to God if his life is ruined through you? Back to your house, Lady Windermere . . . your place is with your child."

The goodness of the play depends on appearances rather than the realities of real lives lived on the cutting edge of passion. Though the play ends happily, it is a happiness compromised with deceit: As critics have often noted, Lady Windermere never discovers the identity of her mother, Lord Windermere never discovers that his wife intended to run away with Lord Darlington, and Lord Augustus never learns the true reason why Mrs. Erlynne was discovered in Lord Darlington's rooms the night before. Everyone is in some essential way ignorant of the truth and perhaps better off for their ignorance — all having been driven to a very hard bargain that they must accept and live with.

A WOMAN OF NO IMPORTANCE

In 1892, after the censorship of *Salomé* and the success of *Lady Windermere's Fan*, Wilde sat down to write *A Woman of No Importance (1893)*. It was commissioned by the actor, playhouse manager, and soon-to-be good friend Herbert Beerbohm Tree for the Haymarket Theatre. *A Woman of No Importance* is a piecemeal play and perhaps one of Wilde's weaker society comedies. Its main redeeming feature, like all of Wilde's drama, is his exquisite use of language and wit.

A Woman of No Importance explores a recurring theme in Wilde's works — the social and ethical implications of a dreadful secret. In this play, Mrs. Arbuthnot, the play's fallen woman, has an illegitimate son, Gerald, who is reunited with his wicked, though charming father, Lord Illingworth. It is no surprise that the theme of illegitimate children and secret family lives intrigued Wilde, who himself was disconnected from his two sons, Vyvyan and Cyril — though he loved them very much. And he was an errant husband, in the model of his own father who had three illegitimate children of his own. Of course, Wilde's adultery was not of the sort that could produce children, but he was drawn to the idea of an identity, a person, being formed as a result of sin, shame, and disgrace.

The reunion of Gerald with his long-lost father Lord Illingworth in *A Woman of No Importance* mirrors that of Lady Windermere and her mother Mrs. Erlynne. But in *A Woman of No Importance*, the identity of the father is revealed to the son. Mrs. Arbuthnot, unlike Mrs. Erlynne, is far more puritanical in her moral conduct now that the stain of her past is behind her. Instead of being outcast from society, she rejects a society that tries to welcome her. In the country houses in which the play is set, many of the aristocratic women ask after Mrs. Arbuthnot and invite her to their parties. It is Mrs. Arbuthnot who rejects them by seldom coming. Having detached herself from society, Mrs. Arbuthnot resents it when her son is about to enter and succeed in the decadent society that was cruel to her in years past. This complication becomes a crisis when the man who is helping Gerald to enter society, Lord Illingworth, is revealed to be Gerald's father. Gerald is forced to choose between a successful career as Lord Illingworth's secretary or love for his mother, which would result in a mediocre and mundane future for him.

To further the drama, Gerald is engaged to Hester, an American woman who is tightly puritanical. She disapproves of all sin, and she loathes the compassion bestowed on sinners, whether they are penitent or not. The life of leisure presented at the beginning of the play is set in direct contrast to the moral ambiguities and complexities that arise at the end. In this way, Wilde again exposes how a complacent society can often mask penetrating and troubling issues that underlie it. Though the play is light in action, it revolves around dialogue, from which readers can tease out some more complicated moral issues. The dialogue itself is lifted mainly from *The Picture of Dorian Gray*, written two years earlier, and Lord Illingworth is an underdeveloped Lord Henry Wotton.

Lord Illingworth is the dandy of the play in his blissful detachment from the action until he is plunged headfirst into it. He then drifts away humiliated when it all is resolved. He makes his glorious debut by responding to the charge that the world thinks him wicked with, "But what world says that, Lady Stutfield? It must be the next world. This world and I are on excellent terms." Like Wilde's typical dandy, he is given to statements like "Nothing is serious except passion. The intellect is not a serious thing, and never has been. It is an instrument on which one plays, that is all." Yet, like Lord Darlington, when he drops the pose of being a dandy and assumes the mask of gravity, he is left the worse for wear. It is typical of Wilde's dandies in his society comedies to lose their identities once they are embroiled in the crisis of the play. In the case of Lord Darlington, self-inflicted exile followed, while Lord Illingworth is banished from the lives of his son and the woman he once loved, Mrs. Arbuthnot.

The moral complexity of the play turns on Mrs. Arbuthnot. She is faced with the dilemma of allowing her son to work for a man, his father, who has done her great evil and who could do the same to her son or preventing him from working for Lord Illingworth and thereby thwarting his dream of becoming a cabinet secretary. In the process of making this decision, she experiences moral growth.

When Hester appeals to Mrs. Arbuthnot, whom she misjudges as equally puritanical, she asks, "A woman who has sinned should be punished, shouldn't she?" Mrs. Arbuthnot agrees with her. The clincher, however, comes later in the dialogue when Mrs. Arbuthnot asks, with a detachment that Hester does not sense though the audience knows full well, "And the children, if there are children, [should they be punished] in the same way also?" The answer is emphatically yes to the Puritan. Mrs. Arbuthnot realizes the extent to which her own Puritanism leads to evil — in punishing both herself and Gerald by making them outcasts in society. She remarks, "It is one of God's terrible laws," as she fades from center stage to the fireplace.

When she is advising Gerald not to take the post as Lord Illingworth's secretary, she makes her only definite moral judgment of the play: Lord Illingworth is a bad man. This is remarkable in Wilde's drama because it is the first time that the dandy is expressly described as wicked. She tells Gerald that Lord Illingworth impregnated "a woman" without marrying her. He promised repeatedly to marry her but never did, until finally she could not bear the disgrace and left. When Gerald remarks that the woman is equally to blame, for "no nice girl" would do that, Mrs. Arbuthnot is struck by her son's hardness and sees that she is partly responsible for her own downfall. She admits this all by granting Gerald permission to work with Lord Illingworth for his professional career.

When afterward, Gerald learns that Lord Illingworth is his father, there is a complex moral moment tucked in the stage directions:

"Gerald clutches his mother's hands and looks into her face. She sinks slowly on the ground in shame. Hester steals toward the door. Lord Illingworth frowns and bites his lip. After a time, Gerald raises his mother up, puts his arm around her, and leads her from the room." Compassion triumphs over Puritanism. Even more penetrating is when Mrs. Arbuthnot, pleadingly, asks Hester again if "the sins of the parents should be visited on the children," Hester says, "I was wrong. God's law is only love."

Though in his own life Wilde usually set ethics and aesthetics against each other, he unites the Christian ethics with the classical aesthetics through love in this play and establishes a universal "higher ethics" that reappears as victorious in all his plays.

AN IDEAL HUSBAND

Unlike its predecessor *A Woman of No Importance*, Wilde's *An Ideal Husband* (1895) cuts straight into action in the first act. The themes are familiar by this point: youthful wrongdoing, secret identities, the error of Puritanism, and the delight of the dandy aesthete. *An Ideal Husband* is probably Wilde's most good-natured play. In its frivolity and affection, it looks forward to Wilde's most renowned play, *The Importance of Being Earnest*. *An Ideal Husband* is quintessential Wilde, with its loving wit, its aesthetic stage directions, and its triviality.

Briefly, the play concerns a married couple, Sir and Lady Chiltern, the dandy Lord Goring, and the woman with a past, Mrs. Cheveley. Lady and Sir Chiltern are happily married, but beneath the veils of a happy marriage is a terrible secret. Sir Chiltern is a very successful and wealthy undersecretary for foreign affairs. His success derives from a very compromising error of his youth: He sold cabinet secrets to a greedy speculator in return for a handsome reward. Many years later, the secret he thought was buried in the past reemerges with the appearance of the seductive, selfish Mrs. Cheveley.

Act One opens with a party in the Chiltern's house. Mrs. Cheveley — as greedy and ambitious as Sir Chiltern was in his youth — plans to blackmail Sir Chiltern with information that she discovered in a letter given to her by the same greedy speculator who tempted Sir Chiltern to error. The speculator was once in love with her. In return for the letter, Mrs. Cheveley wants Sir Chiltern to testify before the House of Commons in favor of a corrupt scheme in which Mrs. Cheveley has a vested financial interest. Mrs. Cheveley understands the gravity of Sir Chiltern's circumstance, the fate of which literally lies in her hands. She rebukes his offer to buy the letter from her with, "Even you are not rich enough, Sir Robert, to buy back your past. No man is." Perhaps he is not, but his conscience is certainly reformed, while Mrs. Cheveley's is not.

Torn between his ambition and his conscience, Sir Robert postpones the decision until his puritanical wife convinces him to refuse Mrs. Cheveley's entreaties. Set against the selfish and amoral Mrs. Cheveley, Lady Chiltern is ridiculously self-righteous on all matters of conscience. When Sir Chiltern pleads that no one should be judged only on the basis of his or her past, Lady Chiltern replies, "One's past is what one is. It is the only way by which people should be judged." Earlier in the play, before the truth of her husband's past is revealed to her, Lady Chiltern talks about evil men who "treat life simply as a sordid speculation." She is not only equating her husband with Mrs. Cheveley, she is signaling her misguided and naïve position to the audience. Clearly, Mrs. Cheveley and Sir Chiltern are two very different moral specimens; something must be amiss in any moral system that places them on equal footing. Assuming that her husband is exonerated from the scandal, she tells him "I will love you always, because you will always be worthy of love." Karl Beckson indicates that in a review of the play written for *The Saturday Review*, playwright George Bernard Shaw noted that "Sir Robert Chiltern's individuality and courage of his wrongdoing as against the mechanical idealism of his stupidly good wife, and his bitter criticism of a love that is only the reward of merit" is the "modern note" of the play.

At this point, Lord Goring, the detached dandy, pokes into the crisis and deflates it. He tries to reason with Sir Chiltern that Lady

Chiltern is imperfect, and allowance of her own imperfections will cause her to forgive her husband's. Lord Goring is the voice of ethical reason, set against Lady Chiltern's hard righteousness and Mrs. Cheveley's decadent selfishness, when he tells Lady Chiltern that "[n]obody is incapable of doing a foolish thing. Nobody is incapable of doing a wrong thing." It is Lord Goring who loosens Lady Chiltern from her zealous Puritanism: The dandy, again, is the force behind ethical change. Once Lady Chiltern has forgiven her husband, and Lord Goring has managed to burn the incriminating letter, he further persuades her to refuse her husband's sacrificial gesture: retiring from public life for good. In this way, Lady Chiltern is making an even bigger sacrifice than her husband was going to make for her. Lord Goring tells her that "[h]e is making for you a terrible sacrifice. Take my advice, Lady Chiltern, and do not accept a sacrifice so great. If you do, you will live to repent it bitterly. We men and women are not made to accept such sacrifices from each other. We are not worthy of them. Besides, Robert has been punished enough."

Lady Chiltern undergoes a radical moral change in this play, while Mrs. Cheveley does not and leaves society disgraced, as the villainous Lord Illingworth did. Like Mrs. Erlynne, Mrs. Cheveley's critical moment in the play results in a burst of passionate love for Lord Goring, who refuses her for the charming Mabel Chiltern, Sir Robert Chiltern's sister. Unlike Mrs. Erlynne, however, her passion is motivated not by self-sacrifice and love but by the selfish desire to use any means to attain her ends. Lady Chiltern, on the contrary, overcomes her mechanical idealism. She allows her husband to continue his successful political career, even if he pursues his ambitions against the wishes of his wife.

Like *A Woman of No Importance*, this play finds a resolution in love. Lady Chiltern ends the play by assuring her husband that she acts out of love, not pity: "It is love, Robert. Love, and only love. For both of us a new life is beginning." In ending with renewal and rebirth, *An Ideal Husband* is one of Wilde's most optimistic dramas. By calling the play *An Ideal Husband*, Wilde was emphasizing that ideals have a terrible uncompromising side to them. Before his secret is revealed, Sir Robert Chiltern is what conventionally would be referred to as an ideal husband. But by play's end, the title role goes to Lord Goring, the philosophical aesthete whose composure and grace cut through an ethical crisis. As Goring's father threatens him at the end of the play, "If you don't make this young lady [Mabel] an ideal husband, I'll cut you off without a shilling." This is Wilde's hint that Goring will indeed make the lovely Mabel an ideal husband. Lucky for Mabel, since her ideal is the aesthetic philosopher it seems: "Geniuses talk so much, don't they? Such a bad habit! And they are always thinking about themselves, when I want them to be thinking about me." She is sure to find such a man in Goring.

When Goring becomes involved in the ethical dilemma, he loses his happy detachment from society and his identity as a dandy, which is signaled by his engagement to Mabel, an official entrance into London's social world. Again, Wilde is challenging societal conventions and putting a puritanical ethical system against an aesthetic one. As always, neither overtly "wins"; rather, both are melded into one another to produce a transcendent morality grounded in charity, love, and forgiveness. That Wilde was struggling with the "Catholic" question his whole life, only to be converted on his deathbed, is no surprise as one reads through his plays, especially one so embedded with the import of Catholic ethical doctrines, like repentance, forgiveness, and salvation as is *An Ideal Husband*.

THE IMPORTANCE OF BEING EARNEST

The Importance of Being Earnest (1895), Wilde's dramatic masterpiece, is more than a mere society comedy. It is a farce. Typical to farces of the time, it proceeds with a tight three-act structure and uses comedy and humor to undercut the dominant culture and cut through artifice. The entire play is a study in absurdity and triviality, with ensuing hilarity.

In his earlier plays, Wilde addressed themes like the hypocrisy of Puritanism in *Lady Windermere's Fan*, incest in *Salomé*, the consequences of excessive passion in *Vera*, and blind selfishness in *An Ideal Husband*. In *The Importance of Being Earnest*, sin and folly are translated into Algy's passion to serve and dine upon cucumber sandwiches ("Speaking of the science of life, have you got the cucumber sandwiches cut?") and his selfish desire for muffins. Vice is not only charming, it is harmless. The deception of leading double lives, which results in tragedy for Dorian Gray, Sir Robert Chiltern, and Mrs. Erlynne, is reduced to the frivolity of "Bunburying." While poking fun at societal morality in this way, Wilde uncovers the void behind it, and the audience cannot help but agree, responding with laughter.

Marriage as well as other traditions of Victorian society, such as teatime, dinner parties, and a correct education, are mocked and trivialized. Wilde characterizes marriage as an encumbrance to the aesthetic lifestyle, which an exchange between Algernon and his butler, Lane, makes eminently clear:

ALGERNON: Why is it that at a bachelor's establishment the servants invariably drink the champagne? I ask merely for information.

LANE: I attribute it to the superior quality of the wine, sir. I have often observed that in married households the champagne is rarely of a first-rate brand.

ALGERNON: Good heavens! Is marriage so demoralizing as that?

Whimsical humor is the answer to lies and manipulation. Sadness is taboo and, more importantly, bad form. The structure of the play is quite simple: Two men would like to marry two women and, after a series of complications, do. The complications are the fun part of the play. The two main characters of the play, Jack and Algernon, have created alter egos. Jack Worthing is Jack in the country and Ernest in the city. As Jack, he tells his niece Cecily and her governess, Ms. Prism, both who live with him in his country house, that he has a wayward brother, Ernest, whom he must tend to in the city. In this way, he escapes dull social engagements in the country and visits his friend Algernon, or Algy, in the city. Similarly, Algy, who lives in the city, has a friend, Bunbury, who lives in the country. Bunbury is an invalid who conveniently needs Algy's nursing and moral support whenever Algy has a dinner engagement with his shrill aunt, Lady Bracknell. Algy's frequent visits to Bunbury prompt Lady Bracknell to remark, "It is very strange. This Mr. Bunbury seems to suffer from curiously bad health." Algy, the dandy supreme, trivializes his lying by calling it "Bunburying."

Lady Bracknell's daughter, Gwendolen, a more developed and conceited Mabel Chiltern, only knows Jack in his Ernest persona. She is the object of Jack's affection, and he hopes to marry her. Lady Bracknell, the embodiment of Victorian convention, however, denies her daughter permission to marry Jack after she learns that he was abandoned as a baby in a handbag at a railway station in London on the Brighton line. When Lady Bracknell learns of his origins, she remarks, "Mr. Worthing, I confess I feel somewhat bewildered by what you have just told me. To be born, or at any rate bred, in a handbag, whether it had handles or not, seems to me to display a contempt for the ordinary decencies of family life that reminds one of the worse excesses of the French Revolution. And I presume you know what that unfortunate movement led to?"

Likewise, Algy is impeded from his matrimonial aims. Algy has heard about Jack's beautiful niece Cecily. He is intrigued by this myste-rious young woman and wants to meet her. But Jack thinks Algy is dis-honest and lecherous and refuses to introduce him to Cecily. Through cunning, Algy manages to visit Jack's country house. While Jack is in town, reputedly "visiting" his wayward brother Ernest, Algy poses as Ernest and travels to the country house to meet Cecily, who is delighted to finally meet her "fiancé," a designation that Algy is not yet aware he has. For some time, Cecily has been intrigued by Jack's alter ego, Ernest, and has created an imaginary romance with him, even fantasizing an engagement.

In the meantime, Jack has decided to end the fiction of Ernest. At about the time Algy arrives at the house impersonating Ernest, Jack returns from London dressed in mourning gear. He has just declared that his brother Ernest has died of a "severe chill" when Algy enters the scene to jubilantly greet his "brother":

CECILY: What is the matter, Uncle Jack? Do look happy! You look as if you had toothache, and I have got such a surprise for you. Who do you think is in the dining room? Your brother!

JACK: Who?

CECILY: Your brother Ernest. He arrived about half an hour ago.

JACK: What nonsense! I haven't got a brother.

CECILY: Oh, don't say that. However badly he may have behaved to you in the past he is still your brother. You couldn't be so heartless as to disown him. I'll tell him to come out. And you will shake hands with him, won't you, Uncle Jack? *(Runs back into the house.)*

CHASUBLE: These are very joyful tidings.

MISS PRISM: After we had all been resigned to his loss, his sudden return seems to me peculiarly distressing.

JACK: My brother is in the dining room? I don't know what it all means. I think it is perfectly absurd.

(Enter Algernon and Cecily hand in hand. They come slowly up to Jack.)

JACK: Good heavens! *(Motions Algernon away.)*

The high-strung Jack insists that Algy leave. As of yet, only the two Bunburyists are aware of the truth of their identities, and Jack is afraid that their secrets will be revealed. A short time later, Gwendolen comes to visit Jack. She meets Cecily first in the garden, and a catty tiff ensues about which one of them is engaged to Ernest. When the ladies discover that neither one of them is engaged to Ernest, they storm outraged out of the garden. As women who have discovered that their lovers are liars, the source of their anger is not what you would expect. They are solely concerned with one seemingly side issue: They will not be marrying a man named Ernest, the importance of which both Gwendolen and Cecily have emphasized to their lovers.

The drama draws to its conclusion with a lucky revelation and an unexpected guest, Lady Bracknell. Algy's aunt is very pleased that Algy and Cecily are getting married as Cecily turns out to be rich. But she still refuses to give Gwendolen permission to marry Jack, who is an orphan and therefore not a worthy husband for her daughter. But it turns out, through a series of revelations, that Jack's mother was Lady Bracknell's sister, which makes Algy — prepare yourself — Jack's younger wayward brother. Excited, Jack says, "I knew I had a brother! I always said I had a brother!" Not only that, Jack, as the elder son, was naturally christened after his father's name, Ernest. The play ends perfectly with Ernest's aunt deriding him, "My nephew, you seem to be displaying signs of triviality." To which Ernest/Jack responds, "On the contrary, Aunt Augusta [Lady Bracknell], I've now realized for the first time in my life the vital importance of being earnest." Here, contradictions do not clash but rather melt into one another, as earnestness and triviality refer to the same thing.

Deception and lies actually are at the service of reality and truth. Typically, as in Wilde's earlier plays, when reality and fiction collide, tragedy and pathos ensue; in *The Importance of Being Earnest*, the result is comedy. What was artificial becomes the guiding principle of life itself, which molds into Wilde's own aesthetic belief that "a truth in art is that whose contradictory is also true," according to Ellmann in the book he edited. The prophesies of Cecily's diary are fulfilled, and it turns out that Jack really is Ernest, which fits into Wilde's aesthetic rule that "life imitates art." Truth is in fact a "morbid and unhealthy" faculty of the mind, while lying is artistic and imaginative. "Things are because we see them, and what we see, and how we see it, depends on the Arts that have influenced us," he writes. The influence of art — of the artificial, the man-made, the fake — abounds in *The Importance of Being Earnest*.

While Algy and Jack are changed by the end of the play, Lady Bracknell remains the same awkward embodiment of Victorian society. Even though she is morally unchanged, her way of living has been overwhelmed by systems that are foreign to her. She, and others like her, are painted as idiotically old-fashioned and obtuse. Miss Prism is another stiff Victorian lady who is unwittingly funny in her judgments and pronouncements. Upon hearing that Jack's brother Ernest has died of a severe chill, she remarks, with Ernest's extravagance and decadence in mind, "What a lesson for him! I hope he will profit by it." Lane, the butler, is dryly witty and evolves beyond the subservient conventions of his post to be a more sympathetic figure than Miss Prism or Lady Bracknell, whom audiences laugh at, not with.

As to the play itself, Wilde wrote that it is "exquisitely trivial, a delicate bubble of fancy, and it has its philosophy . . . that we should treat all the trivial things of life very seriously, and all the serious things with sincere and studied triviality."

The play was adored by audiences and played to packed houses when Wilde's trial began. The torrent of devastatingly bad publicity that ensued unfortunately forced it to close. One of the few critics to savage the play was George Bernard Shaw who wrote that the play was "all froth and no pith," according to Ellmann's biography.

Though sadness is taboo in *The Importance of Being Earnest*, there certainly is a sad irony in the circumstances of Wilde's life at the time.

The society that he was making fun of in his hit play was striking back at him. Where once he pronounced with confidence that the secret of life is art, from prison he would write that "the secret of life is suffering," Ellmann reports in his biography. Still, generations of playgoers will remember the gay Wilde of *The Importance of being Earnest* rather than the broken, spiritless man who died lonely and destitute.

ENTER BOSIE

As Wilde was writing some of the most hilarious comedies of the Victorian age, his personal life was beginning to unravel. The many contradictions of his own psyche and soul clashed not only against each other, but also against the morally rigid society he inhabited. As mentioned earlier, despite being married, Wilde discovered homosexuality at Oxford and indulged in it extramaritally. In 1891, Wilde met the fiery and romantic Alfred "Bosie" Douglas. For two years they were lovers, inseparable until their tempestuous affair was rudely shattered by Wilde's arrest, trial, and conviction for the crime of sodomy. Wilde's accuser was Douglas' father, known to the world as the Marquess of Queensbury, an irascible fellow with whom Douglas was usually at odds.

To say that Douglas and his father had a long and troubled relationship would be an understatement. Douglas used his homosexual relationship with Wilde and Wilde himself as a foil to infuriate his father to the brink of insanity. Wilde later wrote to Douglas, "In your war of hate with your father I was at once shield and weapon to each of you," according to Ellman's biography of Wilde.

To Queensbury, his son's relationship with Wilde was nothing short of repulsive. Hooked on Douglas' bait, he lashed out in a fury. Wilde and Douglas were an item, widely recognized in London's social milieu. Queensbury did not require a private detective or suffer great pains to discover the nature and extent of the affair. He repeatedly warned Douglas to stay away from Wilde, as did Douglas' mother, who wrote in a letter to Douglas quoted by Ellmann in his biography, "If Mr. Wilde has acted as I am convinced he has the part of a Lord Henry Wotton to you I could never feel different towards him than I do, as the murderer of your soul." Still, Douglas remained reckless, apparently determined to wreck himself and Wilde as well.

When Queensbury spied Douglas and Wilde lunching at a café, he posted a letter to Douglas and signed it, "your disgusted so-called father," to which Douglas responded, "What a funny little man you are," according to Ellmann's biography. In response, Queensbury set on a quest to torment Wilde: He would search for Wilde throughout London and when he found him subject him to public humiliation. Wilde, in *De Profundis*, wrote to a friend, "He goes from restaurant to restaurant looking for me, in order to insult me before the whole world, and in such a manner that if I retaliated I would be ruined, and if I did not retaliate I would be ruined also."

In the summer of 1894, Douglas' older brother, Francis Douglas, died under mysterious circumstances — an apparent hunting accident that may have been a suicide. Francis had been given a seat in the House of Lords by the Earl of Rosebery, with whom he was rumored to have had a homosexual relationship. Concerns that this affair would become public, with shameful and even criminal consequences, may have prompted Francis to commit suicide.

Queensbury was intent that his second son not follow the same path. Ellmann indicates that he increased his harassment of Wilde by sending a card to the Albemarle Club, where Wilde dined regularly, that read "To Oscar Wilde, posing Somdomite [*sic*]." After the poisonous card was given to Wilde by an unassuming and embarrassed doorman at the club, Wilde immediately charged Queensberry with libel, with the awareness that evidence could come forth during the libel trail that would precipitate a second trial in which Wilde could be convicted of sodomy. Wilde's friends, including George Bernard Shaw, pleaded with Wilde to drop the case. But Wilde persisted, as if he knew and saw how his tragic life ought to and would unravel before him.

In April, Queensberry was acquitted of libel, and as Wilde had foreseen, the evidence raised at the Queensberry trial made it certain that Wilde would be arrested for homosexual activity. A friendly reporter came to Wilde's apartment and told Robert Ross, who was there with Wilde, that the warrant for Wilde's arrest had just been issued. Anticipating his friends' entreaties that he flee to the continent to avoid the trial, Ellmann's biography quotes Wilde as responding with "I shall stay and do my sentence whatever it is." At this point in his life, Wilde had a sense of foreboding and doom looming over him. He saw a tragic ending as his destiny, and he declined to challenge fate.

On April 26, 1894, Wilde's trial for sodomy and indecency began. The trial resulted in a hung jury, but a second trial was ordered, and this time the verdict was guilty of the counts of indecency and sodomy. Wilde was sentenced to two years of imprisonment at hard labor. Queensbury had made a deal with the prosecutor that if his son's name were kept out of Wilde's trial, Queensbury would help build a winning prosecution by providing powerfully incriminating evidence against Wilde.

Wilde's time in jail was defined by the hard labor that wrecked him physically and surely contributed to his early death. Even as he became physically exhausted in prison, he was also spiritually drained, isolated, and bankrupt. Although initially denied books and writing materials, when his jailers relented, he drew great solace and spiritual revival from Dante's *Divine Comedy*.

On February 16, 1896, during his incarceration, Lady Wilde, Oscar's mother, died. Wilde, possessed of a prophetic sense, knew even before his wife Constance came to Reading Gaol to break the news to him. He had heard the cry of a spider as a warder stepped on it and simultaneously experienced a vision of his mother, dressed as if she were going to town. Wilde asked her to take off her hat and cloak and stay awhile. Instead, she sadly shook her head and faded away. The next day, Constance told Wilde his mother was dead.

DE PROFUNDIS

In 1897, Wilde completed *De Profundis* — an essay written in the form of a letter to Douglas. In it, he details both his own and Douglas' role in his downfall. Though penitent and sorrowful, he did not regret having chosen to live a life of pleasure. He even forgave Douglas for using him as a foil in his ongoing feud with Queensbury.

Wilde also confesses to having acquired humility while in prison and to havelearned that sorrow is the consequence of a complete commitment to the pursuit of pleasure. Thus, for Wilde, the secret of life was no longer art but rather suffering: And then too, there was consolation and redemption.

In *De Profundis*, Wilde writes, "The gods had given me almost everything. But I let myself be lured into long spells of senseless and sensual ease. . . . I grew careless of the lives of others. I took pleasure where it pleased me, and passed on. I forgot that every little action of the common day makes or unmakes character, and that therefore what one has done in the secret chamber one has someday to cry aloud on the housetop. I ceased to be lord over myself. I was no longer the captain of my soul, and did not know it. I allowed pleasure to dominate me. I ended in horrible disgrace. There is only one thing for me now, absolute humility."

In May 1897, Wilde was released from prison. He spent the rest of his life living in poverty in France, Italy, Sicily, and Switzerland. Wilde died in 1900 in Paris at the Hotel d'Alsace, after being received into the Roman Catholic Church. Sick and helpless on his deathbed, Wilde told his good friends Robert Ross and Reggie Turner — the only ones who remained loyal to him throughout his trial and imprisonment — that he had dreamt, a few nights earlier, of supping with the dead. Ellmann reports that Reggie responded "My dear Oscar, you were probably the life and soul of the party."

CONCLUSION

The theme of "Humanitad," the poem that ended his first book of poetry, was that everyone betrays him- or herself. This foreshadows Wilde's own life. And while Wilde was victimized by an age that was intolerant of him, both his life story and his plays remain relevant. Ellmann ends his biography of Wilde by writing, "He belongs to our world more than to Victoria's. Now, beyond the reach of scandal, his best writing validated by time, he comes before us still, a towering figure, laughing and weeping, with parable and paradoxes, so generous, so amusing, and so right."

Wilde's most prolific period of writing was the 1890s, the period after which he decided to pursue men, romantically and sexually, though he was married. While Wilde was enjoying the life of an aesthetic libertine, he was also trying to work out its implications for his work and the consequences it would have both on the society in which he dwelled and on the individuals forced to confront the codes his society lived by. He was to draw his conclusion, with a biblical turn, at the end of *De Profundis*.

> All trials are trials for one's life, just as all sentences are sentences of death; and three times have I been tried. The first time I left the box to be arrested, the second time to be led back to the house of detention, the third time to pass into a prison for two years. Society, as we have constituted it, will have no place for me, has none to offer; but Nature, whose sweet rains fall on unjust and just alike, will have clefts in the rocks where I may hide, and secret valleys in whose silence I may weep undisturbed. She will hang the night with stars so that I may walk abroad in the darkness without stumbling, and send the wind over my footprints so that none may track me to my hurt: she will cleanse me in great waters, and with bitter herbs make me whole.

Perhaps the spirit of Ruskin found him after all — but the spirit of Wilde is the legacy he left behind.

DRAMATIC MOMENTS

from the Major Plays

These short excerpts are from the playwright's major plays. They give a taste of the work of the playwright. Each has a short introduction in brackets that helps the reader understand the context of the excerpt. The excerpts, which are in chronological order, illustrate the main themes mentioned in the In an Hour essay.

CHARACTERS

> Herod
> Salomé
> Herodias
> The Jews

[This one-act play, originally written in French, tells the biblical story of Salomé. In return for performing the dance of the seven veils for Herod, her stepfather, Salomé demands the head of Iokanaan (John the Baptist) on a silver charger.]

HEROD: *(Salomé dances the dance of the seven veils.)* Ah! wonderful! wonderful! You see that she has danced for me, your daughter. Come near, Salomé, come near, that I may give thee thy fee. Ah! I pay a royal price to those who dance for my pleasure. I will pay thee royally. I will give thee whatsoever thy soul desireth. What wouldst thou have? Speak.

SALOMÉ: *(Kneeling.)* I would that they presently bring me in a silver charger . . .

HEROD: *(Laughing.)* In a silver charger? Surely yes, in a silver charger. She is charming, is she not? What is it that thou wouldst have in a silver charger, O sweet and fair Salomé, thou that art fairer than all the daughters of Judea? What wouldst thou have them bring thee in a silver charger? Tell me. Whatsoever it may be, thou shalt receive it. My treasures belong to thee. What is it that thou wouldst have, Salomé?

SALOMÉ: *(Rising.)* The head of Iokanaan.

HERODIAS: Ah! that is well said, my daughter.

HEROD: No, no!

HERODIAS: That is well said, my daughter.

HEROD: No, no, Salomé. It is not that thou desirest. Do not listen to thy mother's voice. She is ever giving thee evil counsel. Do not heed her.

SALOMÉ: It is not my mother's voice that I heed. It is for mine own pleasure that I ask the head of Iokanaan in a silver charger. You have sworn an oath, Herod. Forget not that you have sworn an oath.

HEROD: I know it. I have sworn an oath by my gods. I know it well. But. I pray thee, Salomé, ask of me something else. Ask of me the half of my kingdom, and I will give it thee. But ask not of me what thy lips have asked.

SALOMÉ: I ask of you the head of Iokanaan.

HEROD: No, no, I will not give it thee.

SALOMÉ: You have sworn an oath, Herod.

HERODIAS: Yes, you have sworn an oath. Everybody heard you. You swore it before everybody.

HEROD: Peace, woman! It is not to you I speak.

HERODIAS: My daughter has done well to ask the head of Iokanaan. He has covered me with insults. He has said unspeakable things against me. One can see that she loves her mother well. Do not yield, my daughter. He has sworn an oath, he has sworn an oath.

HEROD: Peace! Speak not to me! . . . Salomé, I pray thee be not stubborn. I have ever been kind toward thee. I have ever loved thee . . . It may be that I have loved thee too much. Therefore ask not this thing of me. This is a terrible thing, an awful thing to ask of me. Surely, I think thou art jesting. The head of a man that is cut from his body is ill to look upon, is it not? It is not meet that the eyes of a virgin should look upon such a thing. What pleasure couldst thou have in it? There is no pleasure that thou couldst have in it. No, no, it is not that thou desirest. Hearken to me. I have an emerald, a great emerald and round, that the minion of Caesar has sent unto me. When thou lookest through this emerald thou canst see that which passeth afar off. Caesar himself carries such an emerald when he goes to the circus. But my emerald is the larger. I know well that it is the larger. It is the largest emerald in the whole world. Thou wilt take that, wilt thou not? Ask it of me and I will give it thee.

SALOMÉ: I demand the head of Iokanaan.

HEROD: Thou art not listening. Thou art not listening. Suffer me to speak, Salomé.

SALOMÉ: The head of Iokanaan!

HEROD: No, no, thou wouldst not have that. Thou sayest that but to trouble me, because that I have looked at thee and ceased not this night. It is true, I have looked at thee and ceased not this night. Thy beauty has troubled me. Thy beauty has grievously troubled me, and I have looked at thee overmuch. Nay, but I will look at thee no more. One should not look at anything. Neither at things, nor at people should one look. Only in mirrors is it well to look, for mirrors do but show us masks. Oh! oh! bring wine! I thirst. . . . Salomé, Salomé, let us be as friends. Bethink thee . . . Ah! what would I say? What was't? Ah! I remember it! . . . Salomé . . . nay but come nearer to me; I fear thou wilt not hear my words. . . . Salomé, thou knowest my white peacocks, my beautiful white peacocks, that walk in the garden between the myrtles and the tall cypress trees. Their beaks are gilded with gold and the grains that they eat are smeared with gold, and their feet are stained with purple. When they cry out the rain comes, and the moon shows herself in the heavens when they spread their tails. Two by two they walk between the cypress trees and the black myrtles, and each has a slave to tend it. Sometimes they fly across the trees, and anon they couch in the grass, and round the pools of the water. There are not in all the world birds so wonderful. I know that Caesar himself has no birds so fair as my birds. I will give thee fifty of my peacocks. They will follow thee whithersoever thou goest, and in the midst of them thou wilt be like unto the moon in the midst of a great white cloud . . . . I will give them to thee, all. I have but a hundred, and in the whole world there is no king who has peacocks like unto my peacocks. But I will give them all to thee. Only thou must loose me from my oath, and must not ask of me that which thy lips have asked of me *(He empties the cup of wine.)*

SALOMÉ: Give me the head of Iokanaan!

HERODIAS: Well said, my daughter! As for you, you are ridiculous with your peacocks.

HEROD: Peace! you are always crying out. You cry out like a beast of prey. You must not cry in such fashion. Your voice wearies me. Peace, I tell you! . . . Salomé, think on what thou art doing. It may be that this man comes from God. He is a holy man. The finger of God has touched him. God has put terrible words into his mouth. In the palace, as in the desert, God is ever with him . . . . It may be that He is, at least. One cannot tell, but it is possible that God is with him and for him. If he die also, peradventure some evil may befall me. Verily, he has said that evil will befall someone on the day whereon he dies. On whom should it fall if it fall not on me? Remember, I slipped in blood when I came hither. Also did I not hear a beating of wings in the air, a beating of vast wings? These are ill omens. And there were other things. I am sure that there were other things, though I saw them not. Thou wouldst not that some evil should befall me, Salomé? Listen to me again.

SALOMÉ: Give me the head of Iokanaan!

HEROD: Ah! thou art not listening to me. Be calm. As for me, am I not calm? I am altogether calm. Listen. I have jewels hidden in this place — jewels that thy mother even has never seen; jewels that are marvelous to look at. I have a collar of pearls, set in four rows. They are like unto moons chained with rays of silver. They are even as half a hundred moons caught in a golden net. On the ivory breast of a queen they have rested. Thou shalt be as fair as a queen when thou wearest them. I have amethysts of two kinds; one that is black like wine, and one that is red like wine that one has coloured with water. I have topazes yellow as are the eyes of tigers, and topazes that are pink as the eyes of a wood-pigeon, and green topazes that are as the eyes of cats. I have opals that burn always, with a flame that is cold as ice, opals that make sad men's minds, and are afraid of the shadows. I have onyxes like the eyeballs of a dead woman. I have moonstones that change when the moon changes, and are wan when they see the sun. I have sapphires big like eggs, and as blue as blue flowers. The sea wanders within them, and the moon comes never to trouble the blue of their waves. I have chrysolites and beryls, and chrysoprases and rubies; I have sardonyx and hyacinth stones, and stones of chalcedony, and I will give them all unto thee, all, and other things will I add to them. The King of the Indies has but even now sent me four fans fashioned from the feathers of parrots, and the King of Numidia a garment of ostrich feathers. I have a crystal, into which it is not lawful for a woman to look, nor may young men behold it until they have been beaten with rods. In a coffer of nacre I have three wondrous turquoises. He who wears them on his forehead can imagine things which are not, and he who carries them in his hand can turn the fruitful woman into a woman that is barren. These are great treasures. They are treasures above all price. But this is not all. In an ebony coffer I have two cups of amber that are like apples of pure gold. If an enemy pour poison into these cups they become like apples of silver. In a coffer incrusted with amber I have sandals incrusted with glass. I have mantles that have been brought from the land of the Serer, and bracelets decked about with carbuncles and with jade that come from the city of Euphrates. . . . What desirest thou more than this, Salomé? Tell me the thing that thou desirest, and I will give it thee. All that thou askest I will give thee, save one thing only. I will give thee all that is mine, save only the life of one man. I will give thee the mantle of the high priest. I will give thee the veil of the sanctuary.

THE JEWS: Oh! oh!

HERODIAS: Give me the head of Iokanaan!

HEROD: *(Sinking back in his seat.)* Let her be given what she asks! Of a truth she is her mother's child. *(The first Soldier approaches. Herodias draws from the hand of the Tetrarch the ring of death, and gives it to the*

Soldier, who straightway bears it to the Executioner. The Executioner looks scared.) Who has taken my ring? There was a ring on my right hand. Who has drunk my wine? There was wine in my cup. It was full of wine. Someone has drunk it! Oh! surely some evil will befall someone. *(The Executioner goes down into the cistern.)* Ah! wherefore did I give my oath? Hereafter let no king swear an oath. If he keep it not, it is terrible, and if he keep it, it is terrible also.

HERODIAS: My daughter has done well.

HEROD: I am sure that some misfortune will happen.

SALOMÉ: *(She leans over the cistern and listens.)* There is no sound. I hear nothing. Why does he not cry out, this man? Ah! if any man sought to kill me, I would cry out, I would struggle, I would not suffer. . . . Strike, strike, Naaman, strike, I tell you. . . . No, I hear nothing. There is a silence, a terrible silence. Ah! something has fallen upon the ground. I heard something fall. It was the sword of the executioner. He is afraid, this slave. He has dropped his sword. He dares not kill him. He is a coward, this slave! Let soldiers be sent. *(She sees the Page of Herodias and addresses him.)* Come hither. Thou wert the friend of him who is dead, wert thou not? Well, I tell thee, there are not dead men enough. Go to the soldiers and bid them go down and bring me the thing I ask, the thing the Tetrarch has promised me, the thing that is mine. *(The Page recoils. She turns to the Soldiers.)* Hither, ye soldiers. Get ye down into this cistern and bring me the head of this man. Tetrarch, Tetrarch, command your soldiers that they bring me the head of Iokanaan. *(A huge black arm, the arm of the Executioner, comes forth from the cistern, bearing on a silver shield the head of Iokanaan. Salomé seizes it. Herod hides his face with his cloak. Herodias smiles and fans herself. The Nazarenes fall on their knees and begin to pray.)*

SALOMÉ: Ah! thou wouldst not suffer me to kiss thy mouth, Iokanaan. Well! I will kiss it now. I will bite it with my teeth as one bites a ripe fruit. Yes, I will kiss thy mouth, Iokanaan. I said it; did I not say it? I said it. Ah! I will kiss it now. . . . But wherefore dost thou not look at me, Iokanaan? Thine eyes that were so terrible, so full of rage and scorn, are shut now. Wherefore are they shut? Open thine eyes! Lift up thine eyelids, Iokanaan! Wherefore dost thou not look at me? Art thou afraid of me, Iokanaan, that thou wilt not look at me? . . . And thy tongue, that was like a red snake darting poison, it moves no more, it speaks no words, Iokanaan, that scarlet viper that spat its venom upon me. It is strange, is it not? How is it that the red viper stirs no longer?. . .Thou wouldst have none of me, Iokanaan. Thou rejectedst me. Thou didst speak evil words against me. Thou didst bear thyself toward me as to a harlot, as to a woman that is a wanton, to me, Salomé, daughter of Herodias, Princess of Judea! Well, I still live, but thou art dead, and thy head belongs to me. I can do with it what I will. I can throw it to the dogs and to the birds of the air. That which the dogs leave, the birds of the air shall devour . . . Ah, Iokanaan, Iokanaan, thou wert the man that I loved alone among men! All other men were hateful to me. But thou wert beautiful! Thy body was a column of ivory set upon feet of silver. It was a garden full of doves and lilies of silver. It was a tower of silver decked with shields of ivory. There was nothing in the world so white as thy body. There was nothing in the world so black as thy hair. In the whole world there was nothing so red as thy mouth. Thy voice was a censer that scattered strange perfumes, and when I looked on thee I heard a strange music. Ah! wherefore didst thou not look at me, Iokanaan? With the cloak of thine hands, and with the cloak of thy blasphemies thou didst hide thy face. Thou didst put upon thine eyes the covering of him who would see his God. Well, thou hast seen thy God, Iokanaan, but me, me, thou didst never see. If thou hadst seen me thou hadst loved me. I saw thee, and I loved thee. Oh, how I loved thee! I love thee yet, Iokanaan. I love only thee . . . I am athirst for thy beauty; I am hungry for thy body; and neither wine nor apples can appease my desire. What shall I do now, Iokanaan? Neither the floods nor the great waters can quench my passion. I was a princess, and thou didst scorn me. I was a virgin, and thou didst take my virginity from me. I was chaste, and thou didst fill my veins with fire . . . Ah! ah! wherefore didst thou not look at me? If thou hadst looked at me thou hadst loved me. Well I know that thou wouldst have loved me, and the mystery of Love is greater than the mystery of Death.

HEROD: She is monstrous, thy daughter; I tell thee she is monstrous. In truth, what she has done is a great crime. I am sure that it is a crime against some unknown God.

HERODIAS: I am well pleased with my daughter. She has done well. And I would stay here now.

HEROD: *(Rising.)* Ah! There speaks my brother's wife! Come! I will not stay in this place. Come, I tell thee. Surely some terrible thing will befall. Manasseh, Issachar, Ozias, put out the torches. I will not look at things, I will not suffer things to look at me. Put out the torches! Hide the moon! Hide the stars! Let us hide ourselves in our palace, Herodias. I begin to be afraid. *(The Slaves put out the torches. The stars disappear. A great cloud crosses the moon and conceals it completely. The stage becomes quite dark. The Tetrarch begins to climb the staircase.)*

THE VOICE OF SALOMÉ: Ah! I have kissed thy mouth, Iokanaan, I have kissed thy mouth. There was a bitter taste on thy lips. Was it the taste of blood? . . . Nay; but perchance it was the taste of love. . . . They say that love hath a bitter taste. But what matter? what matter? I have kissed thy mouth, Iokanaan, I have kissed thy mouth.

(A ray of moonlight falls on Salomé and illumines her.)

HEROD: *(Turning round and seeing Salomé.)* Kill that woman!

(The Soldiers rush forward and crush beneath their shields Salomé, daughter of Herodias, Princess of Judea.)

****

from **Lady Windermere's Fan** (1892)
from Act Three

CHARACTERS

> Mrs. Erlynne
>
> Lady Windermere

[Mistakenly thinking that her husband is having an affair with Mrs. Erlynne, Lady Windermere flees to the house of Lord Darlington, who has recently professed his love for her. Mrs Erlynne arrives and persuades Lady Windermere — her daughter, though Lady Windermere does not know it — to return home to her husband and child.]

MRS. ERLYNNE: Lady Windermere! *(Lady Windermere starts and looks up. Then recoils in contempt.)* Thank Heaven I am in time. You must go back to your husband's house immediately.

LADY WINDERMERE: Must?

MRS. ERLYNNE: *(Authoritatively.)* Yes, you must! There is not a second to be lost. Lord Darlington may return at any moment.

LADY WINDERMERE: Don't come near me!

MRS. ERLYNNE: Oh! You are on the brink of ruin, you are on the brink of a hideous precipice. You must leave this place at once, my carriage is waiting at the corner of the street. You must come with me and drive straight home. *(Lady Windermere throws off her cloak and flings it on the sofa.)* What are you doing?

LADY WINDERMERE: Mrs. Erlynne — if you had not come here, I would have gone back. But now that I see you, I feel that nothing in the whole world would induce me to live under the same roof as Lord Windermere. You fill me with horror. There is something about you that stirs the wildest — rage within me. And I know why you are here. My husband sent you to lure me back that I might serve as a blind to whatever relations exist between you and him.

MRS. ERLYNNE: Oh! You don't think that — you can't.

LADY WINDERMERE: Go back to my husband, Mrs. Erlynne. He belongs to you and not to me. I suppose he is afraid of a scandal. Men are such cowards. They outrage every law of the world, and are afraid of the world's tongue. But he had better prepare himself. He shall have a scandal. He shall have the worst scandal there has been in London for years. He shall see his name in every vile paper, mine on every hideous placard.

MRS. ERLYNNE: No — no —

LADY WINDERMERE: Yes! he shall. Had he come himself, I admit I would have gone back to the life of degradation you and he had prepared for me — I was going back — but to stay himself at home, and to send you as his messenger — oh! it was infamous — infamous.

MRS. ERLYNNE: Lady Windermere, you wrong me horribly — you wrong your husband horribly. He doesn't know you are here — he thinks you are safe in your own house. He thinks you are asleep in your own room. He never read the mad letter you wrote to him!

LADY WINDERMERE: Never read it!

MRS. ERLYNNE: No — he knows nothing about it.

LADY WINDERMERE: How simple you think me! *(Going to her.)* You are lying to me!

MRS. ERLYNNE: *(Restraining herself.)* I am not. I am telling you the truth.

LADY WINDERMERE. If my husband didn't read my letter, how is it that you are here? Who told you I had left the house you were shameless enough to enter? Who told you where I had gone to? My husband told you, and sent you to decoy me back.

MRS. ERLYNNE: *(Right center.)* Your husband has never seen the letter. I — saw it, I opened it. I — read it.

LADY WINDERMERE: *(Turning to her.)* You opened a letter of mine to my husband? You wouldn't dare!

MRS. ERLYNNE. Dare! Oh! to save you from the abyss into which you are falling, there is nothing in the world I would not dare, nothing in the whole world. Here is the letter. Your husband has never read it. He never shall read it. *(Going to fireplace.)* It should never have been written. *(Tears it and throws it into the fire.)*

LADY WINDERMERE: *(With infinite contempt in her voice and look.)* How do I know that that was my letter after all? You seem to think the commonest device can take me in!

MRS. ERLYNNE. Oh! why do you disbelieve everything I tell you? What object do you think I have in coming here, except to save you from utter ruin, to save you from the consequence of a hideous mistake? That letter that is burnt now *was* your letter. I swear it to you!

LADY WINDERMERE: *(Slowly.)* You took good care to burn it before I had examined it. I cannot trust you. You, whose whole life is a lie, could you speak the truth about anything? *(Sits down.)*

MRS. ERLYNNE: *(Hurriedly.)* Think as you like about me — say what you choose against me, but go back, go back to the husband you love.

LADY WINDERMERE: *(Sullenly.)* I do not love him!

MRS. ERLYNNE: You do, and you know that he loves you.

LADY WINDERMERE: He does not understand what love is. He understands it as little as you do — but I see what you want. It would be a great advantage for you to get me back. Dear Heaven! what a life I would have then! Living at the mercy of a woman who has neither mercy nor pity in her, a woman whom it is an infamy to meet, a degradation to know, a vile woman, a woman who comes between husband and wife!

MRS. ERLYNNE: *(With a gesture of despair.)* Lady Windermere, Lady Windermere, don't say such terrible things. You don't know how terrible they are, how terrible and how unjust. Listen, you must listen! Only go back to your husband, and I promise you never to communicate with him again on any pretext — never to see him — never to have anything to do with his life or yours. The money that he gave me, he gave me not through love, but through hatred, not in worship, but in contempt. The hold I have over him —

LADY WINDERMERE: (*Rising.*) Ah! you admit you have a hold!

MRS. ERLYNNE: Yes, and I will tell you what it is. It is his love for you, Lady Windermere.

LADY WINDERMERE: You expect me to believe that?

MRS. ERLYNNE: You must believe it! It is true. It is his love for you that has made him submit to — oh! call it what you like, tyranny, threats, anything you choose. But it is his love for you. His desire to spare you — shame, yes, shame and disgrace.

LADY WINDERMERE: What do you mean? You are insolent! What have I to do with you?

MRS. ERLYNNE: (*Humbly.*) Nothing. I know it — but I tell you that your husband loves you — that you may never meet with such love again in your whole life — that such love you will never meet — and that if you throw it away, the day may come when you will starve for love and it will not be given to you, beg for love and it will be denied you — Oh! Arthur loves you!

LADY WINDERMERE: Arthur? And you tell me there is nothing between you?

MRS. ERLYNNE: Lady Windermere, before Heaven your husband is guiltless of all offence towards you! And I — I tell you that had it ever occurred to me that such a monstrous suspicion would have entered your mind, I would have died rather than have crossed your life or his — oh! died, gladly died!

LADY WINDERMERE: You talk as if you had a heart. Women like you have no hearts. Heart is not in you. You are bought and sold. (*Sits left center.*)

MRS. ERLYNNE: (*Starts, with a gesture of pain. Then restrains herself, and comes over to where Lady Windermere is sitting. As she speaks, she stretches out her hands towards her, but does not dare to touch her.*) Believe what you choose about me. I am not worth a moment's sorrow. But don't spoil your beautiful young life on my account! You don't know what may be in store for you, unless you leave this house at once. You don't know what it is to fall into the pit, to be despised, mocked, abandoned, sneered at — to be an outcast! to find the door shut against one, to have to creep in by hideous byways, afraid every moment lest the mask should be stripped from one's face, and all the while to hear the laughter, the horrible laughter of the world, a thing more tragic than all the tears the world has ever shed. You don't know what it is. One pays for one's sin, and then one pays again, and all one's life one pays. You must never know that. — As for me, if suffering be an expiation, then at this moment I have expiated all my faults, whatever they have been; for tonight you have made a heart in one who had it not, made it and broken it. — But let that pass. I may have wrecked my own life, but I will not let you wreck yours. You — why, you are a mere girl, you would be lost. You haven't got the kind of brains that enables a woman to get back. You have neither the wit nor the courage. You couldn't stand dishonour! No! Go back, Lady Windermere, to the husband who loves you, whom you love. You have a child, Lady Windermere. Go back to that child who even now, in pain or in joy, may be calling to you. *(Lady Windermere rises.)* God gave you that child. He will require from you that you make his life fine, that you watch over him. What answer will you make to God if his life is ruined through you? Back to your house, Lady Windermere — your husband loves you! He has never swerved for a moment from the love he bears you. But even if he had a thousand loves, you must stay with your child. If he was harsh to you, you must stay with your child. If he ill-treated you, you must stay with your child. If he abandoned you, your place is with your child.

(Lady Windermere bursts into tears and buries her face in her hands.)

MRS. ERLYNNE: *(Rushing to her.)* Lady Windermere!

LADY WINDERMERE: *(Holding out her hands to her, helplessly, as a child might do.)* Take me home. Take me home.

MRS. ERLYNNE: *(Is about to embrace her. Then restrains herself. There is a look of wonderful joy in her face.)* Come! Where is your cloak? *(Getting it from sofa.)* Here. Put it on. Come at once!

(They go to the door.)

LADY WINDERMERE: Stop! Don't you hear voices?

MRS. ERLYNNE: No, no! There was no one!

LADY WINDERMERE: Yes, there is! Listen! Oh! that is my husband's voice! He is coming in! Save me! Oh, it's some plot! You have sent for him.

(Voices outside.)

MRS. ERLYNNE: Silence! I'm here to save you, if I can. But I fear it is too late! There! *(Points to the curtain across the window.)* The first chance you have, slip out, if you ever get a chance!

LADY WINDERMERE: But you?

MRS. ERLYNNE: Oh! never mind me. I'll face them.

****

from **An Ideal Husband** (1895)
from Act One

CHARACTERS

> Mabel Chiltern
>
> Lord Goring

[Though this play's plot pivots on corruption and blackmail, this excerpt captures the levity and wit of the Wildean dandy, Lord Goring, as he courts the young and innocent Mabel Chiltern.]

MABEL CHILTERN: You are very late!

LORD GORING: Have you missed me?

MABEL CHILTERN: Awfully!

LORD GORING: Then I am sorry I did not stay away longer. I like being missed.

MABEL CHILTERN: How very selfish of you!

LORD GORING: I am very selfish.

MABEL CHILTERN: You are always telling me of your bad qualities, Lord Goring.

LORD GORING: I have only told you half of them as yet, Miss Mabel!

MABEL CHILTERN: Are the others very bad?

LORD GORING: Quite dreadful! When I think of them at night I go to sleep at once.

MABEL CHILTERN: Well, I delight in your bad qualities. I wouldn't have you part with one of them.

LORD GORING: How very nice of you! But then you are always nice. By the way, I want to ask you a question, Miss Mabel. Who brought Mrs. Cheveley here? That woman in heliotrope, who has just gone out of the room with your brother?

MABEL CHILTERN: Oh, I think Lady Markby brought her. Why do you ask?

LORD GORING: I haven't seen her for years, that is all.

MABEL CHILTERN: What an absurd reason!

LORD GORING: All reasons are absurd.

MABEL CHILTERN: What sort of a woman is she?

LORD GORING: Oh! a genius in the daytime and a beauty at night!

MABEL CHILTERN: I dislike her already.

LORD GORING: That shows your admirable good taste.

****

CHARACTERS

Jack
Gwendolen
Lady Bracknell

[This farce, perhaps the best-known play that Wilde wrote, revolves around mistaken identities, lies, and the hypocrisies of Victorian London. Jack, who is in love with Gwendolen, has devised a fake persona that allows him to escape social obligations. He is Ernest in the city and Jack in the country. His friend, Algernon, quickly follows suit, as is revealed in later scenes.]

JACK: You really love me, Gwendolen?

GWENDOLEN: Passionately!

JACK: Darling! You don't know how happy you've made me.

GWENDOLEN: My own Ernest!

JACK: But you don't really mean to say that you couldn't love me if my name wasn't Ernest?

GWENDOLEN: But your name is Ernest.

JACK: Yes, I know it is. But supposing it was something else? Do you mean to say you couldn't love me then?

GWENDOLEN: *(Glibly.)* Ah! that is clearly a metaphysical speculation, and like most metaphysical speculations has very little reference at all to the actual facts of real life, as we know them.

JACK: Personally, darling, to speak quite candidly, I don't much care about the name of Ernest . . . I don't think the name suits me at all.

GWENDOLEN: It suits you perfectly. It is a divine name. It has a music of its own. It produces vibrations.

JACK: Well, really, Gwendolen, I must say that I think there are lots of other much nicer names. I think Jack, for instance, a charming name.

GWENDOLEN: Jack? . . . No, there is very little music in the name Jack, if any at all, indeed. It does not thrill. It produces absolutely no vibrations . . . I have known several Jacks, and they all, without exception, were more than usually plain. Besides, Jack is a notorious domesticity for John! And I pity any woman who is married to a man called John. She would probably never be allowed to know the entrancing pleasure of a single moment's solitude. The only really safe name is Ernest

JACK: Gwendolen, I must get christened at once — I mean we must get married at once. There is no time to be lost.

GWENDOLEN: Married, Mr. Worthing?

JACK: *(Astounded.)* Well . . . surely. You know that I love you, and you led me to believe, Miss Fairfax, that you were not absolutely indifferent to me.

GWENDOLEN: I adore you. But you haven't proposed to me yet. Nothing has been said at all about marriage. The subject has not even been touched on.

JACK: Well . . . may I propose to you now?

GWENDOLEN: I think it would be an admirable opportunity. And to spare you any possible disappointment, Mr. Worthing, I think it only fair to tell you quite frankly beforehand that I am fully determined to accept you.

JACK: Gwendolen!

GWENDOLEN: Yes, Mr. Worthing, what have you got to say to me?

JACK: You know what I have got to say to you.

GWENDOLEN: Yes, but you don't say it.

JACK: Gwendolen, will you marry me? *(Goes on his knees.)*

GWENDOLEN: Of course I will, darling. How long you have been about it! I am afraid you have had very little experience in how to propose.

JACK: My own one, I have never loved any one in the world but you.

GWENDOLEN: Yes, but men often propose for practice. I know my brother Gerald does. All my girlfriends tell me so. What wonderfully blue eyes you have, Ernest! They are quite, quite, blue. I hope you will always look at me just like that, especially when there are other people present.

(Enter Lady Bracknell.)

LADY BRACKNELL: Mr. Worthing! Rise, sir, from this semi-recumbent posture. It is most indecorous.

GWENDOLEN: Mamma! *(He tries to rise; she restrains him.)* I must beg you to retire. This is no place for you. Besides, Mr. Worthing has not quite finished yet.

LADY BRACKNELL: Finished what, may I ask?

GWENDOLEN: I am engaged to Mr. Worthing, mamma. *(They rise together.)*

LADY BRACKNELL: Pardon me, you are not engaged to anyone. When you do become engaged to someone, I, or your father, should his health permit him, will inform you of the fact. An engagement should come on a young girl as a surprise, pleasant or unpleasant, as the case may be. It is hardly a matter that she could be allowed to arrange for herself. . . . And now I have a few questions to put to you, Mr. Worthing. While I am making these inquiries, you, Gwendolen, will wait for me below in the carriage.

GWENDOLEN: *(Reproachfully.)* Mamma!

LADY BRACKNELL: In the carriage, Gwendolen! *(Gwendolen goes to the door. She and Jack blow kisses to each other behind Lady Bracknell's back. Lady Bracknell looks vaguely about as if she could not understand what the noise was. Finally turns round.)* Gwendolen, the carriage!

GWENDOLEN: Yes, mamma. *(Goes out, looking back at Jack.)*

LADY BRACKNELL: *(Sitting down.)* You can take a seat, Mr. Worthing. *(Looks in her pocket for notebook and pencil.)*

JACK: Thank you, Lady Bracknell, I prefer standing.

LADY BRACKNELL: *(Pencil and notebook in hand.)* I feel bound to tell you that you are not down on my list of eligible young men, although I have the same list as the dear Duchess of Bolton has. We work together, in fact. However, I am quite ready to enter your name, should your answers be what a really affectionate mother requires. Do you smoke?

JACK: Well, yes, I must admit I smoke.

LADY BRACKNELL: I am glad to hear it. A man should always have an occupation of some kind. There are far too many idle men in London as it is. How old are you?

JACK: Twenty-nine.

LADY BRACKNELL: A very good age to be married at. I have always been of opinion that a man who desires to get married should know either everything or nothing. Which do you know?

JACK: *(After some hesitation.)* I know nothing, Lady Bracknell.

LADY BRACKNELL: I am pleased to hear it. I do not approve of anything that tampers with natural ignorance. Ignorance is like a delicate exotic fruit; touch it and the bloom is gone. The whole theory of modern education is radically unsound. Fortunately in England, at any rate, education produces no effect whatsoever. If it did, it would prove a serious danger to the upper classes, and probably lead to acts of violence in Grosvenor Square. What is your income?

JACK: Between seven and eight thousand a year.

LADY BRACKNELL: *(Makes a note in her book.)* In land, or in investments?

JACK: In investments, chiefly.

LADY BRACKNELL: That is satisfactory. What between the duties expected of one during one's lifetime, and the duties exacted from one after one's death, land has ceased to be either a profit or a pleasure. It gives one position, and prevents one from keeping it up. That's all that can be said about land.

JACK: I have a country house with some land, of course, attached to it, about fifteen hundred acres, I believe; but I don't depend on that for my real income. In fact, as far as I can make out, the poachers are the only people who make anything out of it.

LADY BRACKNELL: A country house! How many bedrooms? Well, that point can be cleared up afterwards. You have a town house, I hope? A girl with a simple, unspoiled nature, like Gwendolen, could hardly be expected to reside in the country.

JACK: Well, I own a house in Belgrave Square, but it is let by the year to Lady Bloxham. Of course, I can get it back whenever I like, at six months' notice.

LADY BRACKNELL: Lady Bloxham? I don't know her.

JACK: Oh, she goes about very little. She is a lady considerably advanced in years.

LADY BRACKNELL: Ah, nowadays that is no guarantee of respectability of character. What number in Belgrave Square?

JACK: 149.

LADY BRACKNELL: *(Shaking her head.)* The unfashionable side. I thought there was something. However, that could easily be altered.

JACK. Do you mean the fashion, or the side?

LADY BRACKNELL: *(Sternly.)* Both, if necessary, I presume. What are your polities?

JACK: Well, I am afraid I really have none. I am a Liberal Unionist.

LADY BRACKNELL: Oh, they count as Tories. They dine with us. Or come in the evening, at any rate. Now to minor matters. Are your parents living?

JACK: I have lost both my parents.

LADY BRACKNELL: To lose one parent, Mr. Worthing, may be regarded as a misfortune; to lose both looks like carelessness. Who was your father? He was evidently a man of some wealth. Was he born in what the Radical papers call the purple of commerce, or did he rise from the ranks of the aristocracy?

JACK: I am afraid I really don't know. The fact is, Lady Bracknell, I said I had lost my parents. It would be nearer the truth to say that my parents seem to have lost me. I don't actually know who I am by birth. I was . . . well, I was found.

LADY BRACKNELL: Found!

JACK: The late Mr. Thomas Cardew, an old gentleman of a very charitable and kindly disposition, found me, and gave me the name of Worthing, because he happened to have a first-class ticket for Worthing in his pocket at the time. Worthing is a place in Sussex. It is a seaside resort.

LADY BRACKNELL: Where did the charitable gentleman who had a first-class ticket for this seaside resort find you?

JACK: *(Gravely.)* In a handbag.

LADY BRACKNELL: A handbag?

JACK: *(Very seriously.)* Yes, Lady Bracknell. I was in a handbag — a somewhat large, black leather handbag, with handles to it — an ordinary handbag in fact.

LADY BRACKNELL: In what locality did this Mr. James, or Thomas, Cardew come across this ordinary handbag?

JACK: In the cloakroom at Victoria Station. It was given to him in mistake for his own.

LADY BRACKNELL: The cloakroom at Victoria Station?

JACK: Yes. The Brighton line.

LADY BRACKNELL: The line is immaterial. Mr. Worthing, I confess I feel somewhat bewildered by what you have just told me. To be born, or at any rate bred, in a handbag, whether it had handles or not, seems to me to display a contempt for the ordinary decencies of family life that reminds one of the worst excesses of the French Revolution. And I presume you know what that unfortunate movement led to? As for the particular locality in which the handbag was found, a cloakroom at a railway station might serve to conceal a social indiscretion — has probably, indeed, been used for that purpose before now — but it could hardly be regarded as an assured basis for a recognized position in good society.

JACK: May I ask you then what you would advise me to do? I need hardly say I would do anything in the world to ensure Gwendolen's happiness.

LADY BRACKNELL: I would strongly advise you, Mr. Worthing, to try and acquire some relations as soon as possible, and to make a definite effort to produce at any rate one parent, of either sex, before the season is quite over . . .

****

from **The Importance of Being Earnest** (1895)
from Act Two

CHARACTERS

Jack
Cecily
Gwendolen
Algernon

[Jack and Algernon are revealed as frauds.]

JACK: *(Slowly and hesitatingly.)* Gwendolen — Cecily — it is very painful for me to be forced to speak the truth. It is the first time in my life that I have ever been reduced to such a painful position, and I am really quite inexperienced in doing anything of the kind. However, I will tell you quite frankly that I have no brother Ernest. I have no brother at all. I never had a brother in my life, and I certainly have not the smallest intention of ever having one in the future.

CECILY: *(Surprised.)* No brother at all?

JACK: *(Cheerily.)* None!

GWENDOLEN: *(Severely.)* Had you never a brother of any kind?

JACK: *(Pleasantly.)* Never. Not even of any kind.

GWENDOLEN: I am afraid it is quite clear, Cecily, that neither of us is engaged to be married to anyone.

CECILY: It is not a very pleasant position for a young girl suddenly to find herself in. Is it?

GWENDOLEN: Let us go into the house. They will hardly venture to come after us there.

CECILY: No, men are so cowardly, aren't they?

(They retire into the house with scornful looks.)

JACK: This ghastly state of things is what you call Bunburying, I suppose?

ALGERNON: Yes, and a perfectly wonderful Bunbury it is. The most wonderful Bunbury I have ever had in my life.

JACK: Well, you've no right whatsoever to Bunbury here.

ALGERNON: That is absurd. One has a right to Bunbury anywhere one chooses. Every serious Bunburyist knows that.

JACK: Serious Bunburyist! Good heavens!

ALGERNON: Well, one must be serious about something, if one wants to have any amusement in life. I happen to be serious about Bunburying. What on earth you are serious about I haven't got the remotest idea. About everything, I should fancy. You have such an absolutely trivial nature.

JACK: Well, the only small satisfaction I have in the whole of this wretched business is that your friend Bunbury is quite exploded. You won't be able to run down to the country quite so often as you used to do, dear Algy. And a very good thing too.

ALGERNON: Your brother is a little off colour, isn't he, dear Jack? You won't be able to disappear to London quite so frequently as your wicked custom was. And not a bad thing either.

JACK: As for your conduct towards Miss Cardew, I must say that your taking in a sweet, simple, innocent girl like that is quite inexcusable. To say nothing of the fact that she is my ward.

ALGERNON: I can see no possible defense at all for your deceiving a brilliant, clever, thoroughly experienced young lady like Miss Fairfax. To say nothing of the fact that she is my cousin.

JACK: I wanted to be engaged to Gwendolen, that is all. I love her.

ALGERNON: Well, I simply wanted to be engaged to Cecily. I adore her.

JACK: There is certainly no chance of your marrying Miss Cardew.

ALGERNON: I don't think there is much likelihood, Jack, of you and Miss Fairfax being united.

JACK: Well, that is no business of yours.

ALGERNON: If it was my business, I wouldn't talk about it. *(Begins to eat muffins.)* It is very vulgar to talk about one's business. Only people like stockbrokers do that, and then merely at dinner parties.

JACK: How can you sit there, calmly eating muffins when we are in this horrible trouble, I can't make out. You seem to me to be perfectly heartless.

ALGERNON: Well, I can't eat muffins in an agitated manner. The butter would probably get on my cuffs. One should always eat muffins quite calmly. It is the only way to eat them.

JACK: I say it's perfectly heartless your eating muffins at all, under the circumstances.

ALGERNON: When I am in trouble, eating is the only thing that consoles me. Indeed, when I am in really great trouble, as any one who knows me intimately will tell you, I refuse everything except food and drink. At the present moment I am eating muffins because I am unhappy. Besides, I am particularly fond of muffins. *(Rising.)*

JACK: *(Rising.)* Well, that is no reason why you should eat them all in that greedy way. *(Takes muffins from Algernon.)*

ALGERNON: *(Offering teacake.)* I wish you would have teacake instead. I don't like teacake.

JACK: Good heavens! I suppose a man may eat his own muffins in his own garden.

ALGERNON: But you have just said it was perfectly heartless to eat muffins.

JACK: I said it was perfectly heartless of you, under the circumstances. That is a very different thing.

ALGERNON: That may be. But the muffins are the same. *(He seizes the muffin dish from Jack.)*

JACK: Algy, I wish to goodness you would go.

ALGERNON: You can't possibly ask me to go without having some dinner. It's absurd. I never go without my dinner. No one ever does, except vegetarians and people like that. Besides I have just made arrangements with Dr. Chasuble to be christened at a quarter to six under the name of Ernest.

JACK: My dear fellow, the sooner you give up that nonsense the better.

I made arrangements this morning with Dr. Chasuble to be christened myself at 5.30, and I naturally will take the name of Ernest. Gwendolen would wish it. We can't both be christened Ernest. It's absurd. Besides, I have a perfect right to be christened if I like. There is no evidence at all that I have ever been christened by anybody. I should think it extremely probable I never was, and so does Dr. Chasuble. It is entirely different in your case. You have been christened already.

ALGERNON: Yes, but I have not been christened for years.

JACK: Yes, but you have been christened. That is the important thing.

ALGERNON: Quite so. So I know my constitution can stand it. If you are not quite sure about your ever having been christened, I must say I think it rather dangerous your venturing on it now. It might make you very unwell. You can hardly have forgotten that some one very closely connected with you was very nearly carried off this week in Paris by a severe chill.

JACK: Yes, but you said yourself that a severe chill was not hereditary.

ALGERNON: It usen't to be, I know — but I daresay it is now. Science is always making wonderful improvements in things.

JACK: *(Picking up the muffin dish.)* Oh, that is nonsense; you are always talking nonsense.

ALGERNON: Jack, you are at the muffins again! I wish you wouldn't. There are only two left. *(Takes them.)* I told you I was particularly fond of muffins.

JACK: But I hate teacake.

ALGERNON: Why on earth then do you allow teacake to be served up for your guests? What ideas you have of hospitality!

JACK: Algernon! I have already told you to go. I don't want you here. Why don't you go!

ALGERNON. I haven't quite finished my tea yet! and there is still one muffin left.

(Jack groans, and sinks into a chair. Algernon still continues eating.)

****

from **The Importance of Being Earnest** (1895)
from Act Three

CHARACTERS

> Algernon
> Lady Bracknell
> Cecily
> Jack

[Algernon reveals his engagement to Cecily.]

ALGERNON: I am engaged to be married to Cecily, Aunt Augusta.

LADY BRACKNELL: I beg your pardon?

CECILY: Mr. Moncrieff and I are engaged to be married, Lady Bracknell.

LADY BRACKNELL: *(With a shiver, crossing to the sofa and sitting down.)* I do not know whether there is anything peculiarly exciting in the air of this particular part of Hertfordshire, but the number of engagements that go on seems to me considerably above the proper average that statistics have laid down for our guidance. I think some preliminary inquiry on my part would not be out of place. Mr. Worthing, is Miss Cardew at all connected with any of the larger railway stations in London? I merely desire information. Until yesterday I had no idea that there were any families or persons whose origin was a Terminus.

(Jack looks perfectly furious, but restrains himself.)

JACK: *(In a clear, cold voice.)* Miss Cardew is the granddaughter of the late Mr. Thomas Cardew of 149 Belgrave Square, S.W.; Gervase Park, Dorking, Surrey; and the Sporran, Fifeshire, N.B.

LADY BRACKNELL: That sounds not unsatisfactory. Three addresses always inspire confidence, even in tradesmen. But what proof have I of their authenticity?

JACK. I have carefully preserved the Court Guides of the period. They are open to your inspection, Lady Bracknell.

LADY BRACKNELL: *(Grimly.)* I have known strange errors in that publication.

JACK: Miss Cardew's family solicitors are Messrs. Markby, Markby, and Markby.

LADY BRACKNELL: Markby, Markby, and Markby? A firm of the very highest position in their profession. Indeed I am told that one of the Mr. Markby's is occasionally to be seen at dinner parties. So far I am satisfied.

JACK: *(Very irritably.)* How extremely kind of you, Lady Bracknell! I have also in my possession, you will be pleased to hear, certificates of Miss Cardew's birth, baptism, whooping cough, registration, vaccination, confirmation, and the measles; both the German and the English variety.

LADY BRACKNELL: Ah! A life crowded with incident, I see; though perhaps somewhat too exciting for a young girl. I am not myself in favour of premature experiences. *(Rises, looks at her watch.)* Gwendolen! the time approaches for our departure. We have not a moment to lose. As a matter of form, Mr. Worthing, I had better ask you if Miss Cardew has any little fortune?

JACK: Oh! about a hundred and thirty thousand pounds in the Funds. That is all. Goodbye, Lady Bracknell. So pleased to have seen you.

LADY BRACKNELL: *(Sitting down again.)* A moment, Mr. Worthing. A hundred and thirty thousand pounds! And in the Funds! Miss Cardew seems to me a most attractive young lady, now that I look at her. Few girls of the present day have any really solid qualities, any of the qualities that last, and improve with time. We live, I regret to say, in an age of surfaces. *(To Cecily.)* Come over here, dear. *(Cecily goes across.)* Pretty child! your dress is sadly simple, and your hair seems almost as Nature might have left it. But we can soon alter all that. A thoroughly experienced French maid produces a really marvelous result in a very brief space of time. I remember recommending one to young Lady Lancing, and after three months her own husband did not know her.

JACK: And after six months nobody knew her.

LADY BRACKNELL: *(Glares at Jack for a few moments. Then bends, with a practiced smile, to Cecily.)* Kindly turn round, sweet child. *(Cecily turns completely round.)* No, the side view is what I want. *(Cecily presents her profile.)* Yes, quite as I expected. There are distinct social possibilities in your profile. The two weak points in our age are its want of principle and its want of profile. The chin a little higher, dear. Style largely depends on the way the chin is worn. They are worn very high, just at present. Algernon!

ALGERNON: Yes, Aunt Augusta!

LADY BRACKNELL: There are distinct social possibilities in Miss Cardew's profile.

ALGERNON: Cecily is the sweetest, dearest, prettiest girl in the whole world. And I don't care twopence about social possibilities.

LADY BRACKNELL: Never speak disrespectfully of Society, Algernon. Only people who can't get into it do that. *(To Cecily.)* Dear child, of course you know that Algernon has nothing but his debts to depend upon. But I do not approve of mercenary marriages. When I married Lord Bracknell I had no fortune of any kind. But I never dreamed for a moment of allowing that to stand in my way. Well, I suppose I must give my consent.

ALGERNON: Thank you, Aunt Augusta.

LADY BRACKNELL: Cecily, you may kiss me!

CECILY: *(Kisses her.)* Thank you, Lady Bracknell.

LADY BRACKNELL: You may also address me as Aunt Augusta for the future.

CECILY: Thank you, Aunt Augusta.

LADY BRACKNELL: The marriage, I think, had better take place quite soon.

ALGERNON: Thank you, Aunt Augusta.

CECILY: Thank you, Aunt Augusta.

LADY BRACKNELL: To speak frankly, I am not in favour of long engagements. They give people the opportunity of finding out each other's character before marriage, which I think is never advisable.

JACK: I beg your pardon for interrupting you, Lady Bracknell, but this engagement is quite out of the question. I am Miss Cardew's guardian, and she cannot marry without my consent until she comes of age. That consent I absolutely decline to give.

LADY BRACKNELL: Upon what grounds may I ask? Algernon is an extremely, I may almost say an ostentatiously, eligible young man. He has nothing, but he looks everything. What more can one desire?

JACK: It pains me very much to have to speak frankly to you, Lady Bracknell, about your nephew, but the fact is that I do not approve at all of his moral character. I suspect him of being untruthful. *(Algernon and Cecily look at him in indignant amazement.)*

LADY BRACKNELL: Untruthful! My nephew Algernon? Impossible! He is an Oxonian.

JACK: I fear there can be no possible doubt about the matter. This afternoon during my temporary absence in London on an important question of romance, he obtained admission to my house by means of the false pretence of being my brother. Under an assumed name he drank, I've just been informed by my butler, an entire pint bottle of my Perrier-Jouet, Brut, '89; wine I was specially reserving for myself. Continuing his disgraceful deception, he succeeded in the course of the afternoon in alienating the affections of my only ward. He subsequently stayed to tea, and devoured every single muffin. And what makes his conduct all the more heartless is, that he was perfectly well aware from the first that I have no brother, that I never had a brother, and that I don't intend to have a brother, not even of any kind. I distinctly told him so myself yesterday afternoon.

LADY BRACKNELL: Ahem! Mr. Worthing, after careful consideration I have decided entirely to overlook my nephew's conduct to you.

JACK: That is very generous of you, Lady Bracknell. My own decision, however, is unalterable. I decline to give my consent.

LADY BRACKNELL: *(To Cecily.)* Come here, sweet child. *(Cecily goes over.)* How old are you, dear?

CECILY: Well, I am really only eighteen, but I always admit to twenty when I go to evening parties.

LADY BRACKNELL: You are perfectly right in making some slight alteration. Indeed, no woman should ever be quite accurate about her age. It looks so calculating . . . *(In a meditative manner.)* Eighteen, but admitting to twenty at evening parties. Well, it will not be very long before you are of age and free from the restraints of tutelage. So I don't think your guardian's consent is, after all, a matter of any importance.

JACK: Pray excuse me, Lady Bracknell, for interrupting you again, but it is only fair to tell you that according to the terms of her grandfather's will Miss Cardew does not come legally of age till she is thirty-five.

LADY BRACKNELL: That does not seem to me to be a grave objection. Thirty-five is a very attractive age. London society is full of women of the very highest birth who have, of their own free choice, remained thirty-five for years. Lady Dumbleton is an instance in point. To my own knowledge she has been thirty-five ever since she arrived at the age of forty, which was many years ago now. I see no reason why our dear Cecily should not be even still more attractive at the age you mention than she is at present. There will be a large accumulation of property.

CECILY: Algy, could you wait for me till I was thirty-five?

ALGERNON: Of course I could, Cecily. You know I could.

CECILY: Yes, I felt it instinctively, but I couldn't wait all that time. I hate waiting even five minutes for anybody. It always makes me rather cross. I am not punctual myself, I know, but I do like punctuality in others, and waiting, even to be married, is quite out of the question.

ALGERNON: Then what is to be done, Cecily?

CECILY: I don't know, Mr. Moncrieff.

LADY BRACKNELL: My dear Mr. Worthing, as Miss Cardew states positively that she cannot wait till she is thirty-five — a remark which I am bound to say seems to me to show a somewhat impatient nature — I would beg of you to reconsider your decision.

JACK: But my dear Lady Bracknell, the matter is entirely in your own hands. The moment you consent to my marriage with Gwendolen, I will most gladly allow your nephew to form an alliance with my ward.

LADY BRACKNELL: *(Rising and drawing herself up.)* You must be quite aware that what you propose is out of the question.

JACK: Then a passionate celibacy is all that any of us can look forward to.

LADY BRACKNELL: That is not the destiny I propose for Gwendolen. Algernon, of course, can choose for himself. *(Pulls out her watch.)* Come, dear, *(Gwendolen rises.)* we have already missed five, if not six, trains. To miss any more might expose us to comment on the platform.

****

Wilde

THE READING ROOM

YOUNG ACTORS AND THEIR TEACHERS

Bloom, Harold, ed. *The Literary Criticism of John Ruskin*. New York: Da Capo Press, 1987.

_____. *The Importance of Being Earnest: Modern Critical Interpretations*. New York: Chelsea House Publishers, 1988.

Coakley, Davis. *Oscar Wilde: the Importance of Being Irish*. Dublin: Town House, 1994.

Cohen, Philip K. *The Moral Vision of Oscar Wilde*. Rutherford, N.J.: Fairleigh Dickinson University Press, 1978.

_____. *Oscar Wilde*. London: Hamish Hamilton, 1987.

Gagnier, Regenia, ed. *Critical Essays on Oscar Wilde*. New York: Maxwell Macmillan International, 1991.

Hyde, H. Montgomery, ed. *The Three Trials of Oscar Wilde*. New York: University Books, 1956.

Knox, Melissa. *Oscar Wilde: A Long and Lovely Suicide*. New Haven, Conn.: Yale University Press, 1994.

Lloyd, Rosemary, ed. *The Cambridge Companion to Baudelaire*. Cambridge: Cambridge University Press, 2005.

Pearson, Hesketh. *Oscar Wilde: His Life and Wit*. New York: Grosset & Dunlap, 1946.

Woodcock, George. *The Paradox of Oscar Wilde*. London: T. V. Boardman, 1949.

SCHOLARS, STUDENTS, PROFESSORS

Bashford, Bruce. *Oscar Wilde: The Critic as Humanist*. Rutherford, N.J.: Fairleigh Dickinson University Press, 1999.

Birkett, Jennifer. *The Sins of the Fathers: Decadence in France 1870–1914*. London: Quartet Books, 1986.

Casteras, Susan P., ed. *John Ruskin and the Victorian Eye*. New York: Harry N. Abrams, 1993.

This extensive bibliography lists books about the playwright according to whom the books might be of interest. If you would like to research further something that interests you in the text, lists of references, sources cited, and editions used in this book are found in this section.

Craig, David M. *John Ruskin and the Ethics of Consumption*. Charlottesville: University of Virginia Press, 2006.

Edwards, Jason. *Alfred Gilbert's Aestheticism: Gilbert Amongst Whistler, Wilde, Leighton, Pater and Burne-Jones*. Aldershot, Hampshire, UK: Ashgate, 2006.

Feldman, Jessica R. *Gender on the Divide: The Dandy in Modernist Literature*. Ithaca, N.Y.: Cornell University Press, London 1993.

Gillespie, Michael Patrick. *Oscar Wilde and the Poetics of Ambiguity*. Gainesville: University Press of Florida, 1996.

Killeen, Jarlath. *The Faiths of Oscar Wilde: Catholicism, Folklore and Ireland*. New York: Palgrave Macmillan, 2005.

Nahum, Peter, ed. *Burne-Jones, the Pre-Raphaelites and Their Century*. London: Peter Nahum, 1989.

Nassaar, Christopher S. *Into the Demon Universe: A Literary Exploration of Oscar Wilde*. New Haven: Yale University Press, 1974.

Prettejohn, Elizabeth, ed. *After the Pre-Raphaelites: Art and Aestheticism in Victorian England*. Manchester, UK: Manchester University Press, 1999.

_____. *The Art of the Pre-Raphaelites*. London: Tate Publishing, 2000.

Raby, Peter. *Oscar Wilde*. Cambridge: Cambridge University Press, 1997.

Sherard, Robert H. *Oscar Wilde: The Story of an Unhappy Friendship*. London: Greening & Company, 1909.

Shewan, Rodney. *Oscar Wilde: Art and Egotism*. New York: Barnes & Noble Books, 1977.

THEATER, PRODUCERS

Douglas, Alfred D. *Oscar Wilde; A Summing-Up*. London: Duckworth, 1940.

Eltis, Sos. *Revising Wilde: Society and Subversion in the Plays of Oscar Wilde*. Oxford: Clarendon Press, 1996.

Gagnier, Regenia A. *Idylls of the Marketplace: Oscar Wilde and the Victorian Public*. London: Scholar, 1987.

Holland, Merlin, ed. *Oscar Wilde: A Life in Letters*. New York: Carroll & Graf, 2007.

Morgan, Margery M. *File on Wilde*. London: Methuen, 1990.

Tydeman, William, ed. *Wilde Comedies: Lady Windermere's Fan, A Woman of No Importance, An Ideal Husband, The Importance of Being Earnest: A Casebook.* London: Macmillan, 1982.

Tydeman, William, and Steven Price. *Wilde: Salome (Plays in Production).* Cambridge: Cambridge University Press, 1996.

Winwar, Frances. *Oscar Wilde and the Yellow Nineties.* New York: Harper, 1940.

ACTORS, DIRECTORS, THEATER PROFESSIONALS

Guy, Josephine M., and Ian Small. *Oscar Wilde's Profession: Writing and the Culture of Industry in the Late Nineteenth Century.* Oxford: Oxford University Press, 2000.

Jackson, Allan Stuart. *The Standard Theatre of Victorian England.* Rutherford, N.J.: Fairleigh Dickinson University Press, 1993.

Jackson, Russell, ed. *Victorian Theatre: The Theatre in its Time.* New York: New Amsterdam, 1989.

Jackson, Russell, and Ian Small, eds. *The Complete Works of Oscar Wilde.* New York: Oxford University Press, 2000.

Kaplan, Joel H. et al. *Theatre and Fashion: Oscar Wilde to the Suffragettes.* Cambridge: Cambridge University Press, 1994.

Keane, Robert, ed. *Oscar Wilde: The Man, his Writings, and His World.* New York: AMS Press, 2003.

Nicoll, Allardyce. *A History of Late Nineteenth Century Drama, 1850–1900.* Cambridge: Cambridge University Press, 1946.

Powell, Kerry. *Oscar Wilde and the Theatre of the 1890s.* Cambridge: Cambridge University Press, 1990.

Rowell, George. *The Victorian Theatre, 1792–1914: A Survey.* Cambridge: Cambridge University Press, 1978.

Sammells, Neil. *Wilde Style: The Plays and Prose of Oscar Wilde.* Harlow, Essex, UK: Pearson Education, 2000.

Smith, Philip E., II, and Michael S. Helfand, eds. *Oscar Wilde's Oxford Notebooks: A Portrait of Mind in the Making.* New York: Oxford University Press, 1989.

Varty, Anne. *A Preface to Oscar Wilde.* Harlow, Essex, UK: Longman, 1998.
_____. *The Plays of Oscar Wilde.* Hertfordshire, UK: Wordsworth Classics, 2002.

Wilde, Oscar. *Plays, Prose Writings and Poems*. New York: Everyman's Library, 1991.

THE EDITIONS OF WILDE'S WORKS USED FOR THIS BOOK

The works of Oscar Wilde are in the public domain and can be accessed at: http://onlinebooks.library.upenn.edu/webbin/book/lookupname? key=Wilde%2c%20Oscar%2c%201854-1900

SOURCES CITED IN THIS BOOK

Beckson, Karl, ed. *Oscar Wilde: The Critical Heritage*. New York: Barnes & Noble, 1970.

Ellmann, Richard, ed. *Oscar Wilde: A Collection of Critical Essays*. Englewood Cliffs, N.J.: Prentice-Hall, 1969.

Ellmann, Richard. *Oscar Wilde*. London: Hamish Hamilton, 1987.

Harris, Frank. *Oscar Wilde: His Life and Confessions*. New York: Covici, Friede, 1930.

McKenna, Neil. *The Secret Life of Oscar Wilde*. London: Century, 2003.

Pater, Walter. *Walter Pater: Three Major Texts (The Renaissance, Appreciations, and Imaginary Portraits)*. Edited by William E. Buckler. New York: New York University Press, 1986.

Pearce, Joseph. *The Unmasking of Oscar Wilde*. London: HarperCollins, 2000.

Raby, Peter, ed. *The Cambridge Companion to Oscar Wilde*. Cambridge: Cambridge University Press, 1997.

Tree, Herbert Beerbohm quoted at www.archive.org/stream/cu3192401 3232347/cu31924013232347_djvu.txt

Wilde, Oscar. *The Artist as Critic: Critical Writings of Oscar Wilde*. Edited by Richard Ellmann. Chicago: University of Chicago, 1982.

_____. *De Profundis*. Mineola, N.Y.: Dover Publications, 1996.

_____. *The Plays of Oscar Wilde*. Hertfordshire, UK: Wordsworth Editions, 2002.

Zukowski, Karen. *Creating the Artful Home: The Aesthetic Movement*. Layton, Utah: Gibbs Smith, 2006.

INDEX

The entries in the index include highlights from the main In an Hour essay portion of the book.

Know the playwright, love the play.

Open a new door to theater study, performance, and audience satisfaction with these Playwrights In an Hour titles.

ANCIENT GREEK

Aeschylus   Aristophanes   Euripides   Sophocles

RENAISSANCE

William Shakespeare

MODERN

Anton Chekhov   Noël Coward   Lorraine Hansberry
Henrik Ibsen   Arthur Miller   Molière   Eugene O'Neill
Arthur Schnitzler   George Bernard Shaw   August Strindberg
Frank Wedekind   Oscar Wilde   Thornton Wilder
Tennessee Williams

CONTEMPORARY

Edward Albee   Alan Ayckbourn   Samuel Beckett
Theresa Rebeck   Sarah Ruhl   Sam Shepard   Tom Stoppard
August Wilson

To purchase or for more information
visit our web site inanhourbooks.com

ABOUT THE AUTHOR

Emily Esfahani Smith, a recent graduate of Dartmouth College, is a journalist and writer in Washington, D.C. Her work on cultural, political, and international affairs has appeared in *The Wall Street Journal, The Weekly Standard, National Review, The American Spectator,* and *The New Criterion.*